To Dori

from

mikle Dorn

As I Saw It

The Inside Story *of the* Golden Years *of* Television

By Mike Dann

As told to Paul Berger

MikeDannAsISawIt.com

LEVINE MESA
PRESS

LevineMesaPress.com
El Prado, New Mexico

Published by:
Levine Mesa Press
PO Box 2218
El Prado, NM 87529

LEVINE MESA
PRESS

LevineMesaPress.com

ISBN: 978-0-9823887-1-6

Library of Congress Control Number: 2009925914

This book is printed on acid-free paper.

Printed in the United States of America

To Pete Seeger,

who gave me the knowledge and the courage for all the things he fought for and achieved and whom I met on rare occasions because of the Smothers Brothers Comedy Hour.

And to David Halberstam,

whom I liked to say was one of my very best friends.

"The change to the Wired Society, with the advent of cable and fiber optics, was not like going from the propeller to the jet. It was like going from the horse to the combustible engine. It changed society completely."
— Mike Dann, teaching "The Wired Society," Yale, circa 1970.

Table of Contents

Preface

This is the story of one of the most powerful men in network television. Judy Garland performed in his office, Danny Kaye cooked dinner for him, Lucille Ball looked after him like a son and a U.S. President tried to control his biggest hit program. Over the course of his career he worked for some of the greatest television executives this country has ever seen and some tyrants too—media moguls, visionaries and one closely related to the mob.

Every week for more than 20 years he faced the challenge of deciding which programs millions of Americans would watch on their television screens. He was responsible for some of TV's greatest moments: Hal Holbrook in Mark Twain, Sir Lawrence Olivier's Richard III, The Defenders, the Smothers Brothers and Mary Tyler Moore. But he also perpetuated some of its most populist forms: The Beverly Hillbillies, The Munsters and Gentle Ben.

He was not a creative man. Nor was he a television prophet. He was an executive. A bureaucrat. A suit. It was, perhaps, the most exciting career such a man could wish for—a suite at the Beverly Hills Hotel; a private screening room and a personal chef; lunches and dinners at Le Pavillon and The Four Seasons; a limitless expense account; and a line of girls trailing out his office door, who all thought he was the tallest, handsomest, funniest man they had ever seen.

Of course, he wasn't. He was a short Jewish guy from Detroit—good-looking but with a limp after an attack of polio in his youth—who just happened to control hundreds of millions of annual programming dollars for the most powerful and successful television network in American history: CBS.

At the apogee of his network power during the 1960s, he headed one of the most creative programming teams ever assembled. Guided by his instincts, he steered them to ratings victory year after year. Unlike many of his peers, he never hungered for the top job: network president. His focus was on one simple goal: to win—and win at all costs.

In the coming pages we will trace the metamorphosis of this man, from a junior employee in the press department of NBC to one of the most successful network programming heads America has ever seen.

He was the right man in the right industry at the right time.

His name was Myron Harold Dann—Mike Dann to those who knew him. This is his story. This is television. Now let's get on with the show.

Paul Berger

I.

Under Pressure

"This instrument can teach, it can illuminate; yes, and it can even inspire. But it can do so only to the extent that humans are determined to use it to those ends. Otherwise it is merely wires and lights in a box." – Edward R. Murrow, speech to annual convention of the Radio and Television News Directors Association, Chicago, October 15, 1958.

"If you've got enough winners you can do whatever you want. But without commercial success on a network you're no place." – Mike Dann, speech to the National Association of Television Program Executives, circa 1958.

From my office on the 34th floor of the Columbia Broadcasting System (CBS) headquarters in midtown New York, I could see clear across Manhattan: the Chrysler Building glinting in the early spring sunshine to the southeast, the pulsating blue insignia of the rival American Broadcasting Company (ABC) a couple of blocks north at 54th Street and, further north still, the tree-lined oasis of Central Park. It was Thursday, March 5, 1970, and although I was one of the most powerful television executives in America, I awaited the arrival of the reporter from Variety like a nervous teen.

I had spent more than 20 years in the television industry, the last 12 of them at CBS where I had been consumed by the task of programming what was then the most successful television network in American history. CBS had topped the ratings for the past 14 years, with the National Broadcasting Company (NBC) never far behind. But in February 1970, Variety published a story predicting the end of CBS's reign under the headline "NBC's Edge of Nighttime." The piece concluded that CBS was doing so badly that the odds of winning the 1969-70 season were hopeless. If correct, it all but ensured the end of my CBS career. So I had called the Variety reporter, Les Brown, at his home and invited him up to my office to persuade him he was wrong.

It was early afternoon and the lights on the five-unit telephone console that sat on my desk were uncharacteristically dark. I had instructed Madeline Katz, my secretary, to hold all my calls. I had been working 17 hours a day since the beginning of January and it showed. My usually tanned skin was dull and life-less, and I had spent so long barking at agents, producers and executives that my voice was hoarse. Brown would later note that I looked a good deal older than my 48 years.

I turned away from the window and slumped into my chair, swiveling 360 degrees while pushing the eraser end of a pencil into my ear—one of the many nervous tics I acquired over the years. There was a knock on the door, and Madeline entered the room with Brown trailing behind. I yanked the pencil away from my head, jumped to my feet and hurried over to thank Brown for coming at such short notice.

I had first met Brown about five years earlier when he replaced Variety's then TV editor George Rosen. Variety might not have carried the same weight as a piece in The New York Times. But it was the industry publication, and I cared a great deal when anything derogatory was written about CBS, particularly about me, within its imposing broadsheet pages.

After welcoming Brown into my office, I guided him across the room where I directed his attention to a piece of cream-colored paper taped to the wall. Across the top of the paper in red ink was the title: "OPERATION 100 (JANUARY 10-APRIL 19, 1970)." I walked behind my large walnut desk, paused for a moment to let the gravity of what Brown was about to hear sink in, and then began a detailed explanation of the purpose of my invitation.

Brown had indeed been correct about CBS's programming woes. We were doing terribly. And millions of viewers and hundreds of millions of dollars were at stake. Schedules are laid out in the winter. They debut in the fall and they end in the spring. When I set the CBS 1969-70 schedule, I had made very few changes from the previous winning year, which had consisted mainly of hour-long variety programs and 30-minute sitcoms. Yet for the first three months of the season, hundreds of thousands of television viewers had voted with their dials, choosing NBC over CBS. Operation 100 was my master plan to win them back in time for the ratings close on April 19.

The concept was simple: Rip up the schedule in January and for the last 100 days counter-program the hell out of NBC, substituting failing shows with one-off specials, comedy repeats, documentaries and movies. TV Guide had to rewrite a lot of magazines.

As I explained to Brown that the pressure had been immense my voice cracked. I told him that I had never lost a season, that this could possibly be my final year at CBS, and that I was damned if I was going to lose now. I told him that our network president, Bob Wood, had given me the all clear and that

I had instructed my staff they were to do whatever it took to win. We knew which shows to replace—the A.C. Nielsen Company had registered their poor performance throughout the fall. But in order to work out which shows to put on in their place, we had to know what the competition was doing as well. So since the beginning of the New Year, my staff and I had begged and cajoled our contacts in the advertising industry to reveal NBC's entire schedule for the upcoming months.

I stuffed a file of papers in Brown's hands containing the notes, ideas and shows my staff in New York and L.A. had compiled to beat NBC. I started out in television with dreams of bringing art and culture to the masses. But in attempting to lead CBS to victory for an unprecedented 15th year I was relying on aging stars like Jackie Gleason and Red Skelton, on documentary shows with sensationalist titles like *Eskimo: Fight for Life*, and on movie reruns like *The African Queen* and *Born Free*. Brown seemed almost amused at the lengths to which we had gone to claw back the ratings. Exhausted and at my wits' end, something snapped.

"Who is hurt by this?" I yelled at Brown, who dutifully recorded the tirade in a book, *Television: The Business Behind the Box*, which appeared a year later. "The public? Are they better off with my educational Eskimo film or that Tim Conway crap that nobody likes? Are they better off with more jugglers and bum comedians on Sullivan or that show we're doing from the veterans' hospital? Tell me that we sold the kids short by giving them *Born Free* and *Lions Are Free*. Okay, so it's a repeat. The kids who saw it this time were sucking a tit the last time it played."

Coarse, I know. But this was the culmination of almost 22 years spent working under unbearable pressure. I had survived longer at the top than every one of my peers. My previous bosses had been a succession of putzes, with the exception of a tyrannical, womanizing bully with ties to the mob, who was known affectionately around the office as the "Smiling Cobra." When I was not on one of my frequent trips to Hollywood, I spent lunchtimes on the couch of one of New York's foremost psychoanalysts. I was taking three pills a day for high blood pressure, stress and insomnia. My greatest triumphs had largely been celebrated alone. My wife hated television.

Not that I am trying to depict myself as a martyr. I was a front-line fighter in the ratings wars, and I would trample on anything and anyone to succeed. Did I lie? Sure. Was I rude? Yes. But I never sacrificed my integrity. I never got involved in scandal. I never took a dollar for payment. I never cheated or stole or accepted a bribe. I refused hundreds of millions of dollars; not because I was moral, but because my reputation was at stake and I could not live with myself, or face my family, if I took a dime.

Every spring for almost 10 years, directly or indirectly, I hired and fired thousands of people as I studied ratings and budgets, sat through endless pilots and argued over which shows would go on the air and which would come off. Producers of great wealth stormed into my office with promises and threats. Powerful people vowed never to talk to me again. But it was television. My success and failure depended upon the ratings. I could not afford to put on a show because the producer was a friend or offered money, or both—not because I had moral character but because if anybody ever found out my career would have been destroyed. The only yardstick I needed to measure the worth of a show was the ratings.

I was completely driven by numbers. I lived or died by them. My desire might have been to pioneer better programming, but I became part of the system that broke it. My commanding philosophy was: If you've got enough winners you can do whatever you want. But without commercial success on a network you're no place. Sometimes I had wonderful shows with talented people, but the audience never came. Other times I had shows that were perfectly awful, but the audience loved them so they stayed.

That was the entire ethos behind the 100 Days. It was a statistical race based on raw data from a few thousand homes scattered across America and watched over by that soulless monolith, the A.C. Nielsen Company. It was of huge importance, not just for me but also for the network, for our advertisers, for our affiliates and for the hundreds of people who worked on our shows. Those Nielsen numbers decided which shows lived and which shows died, which advertisers would choose CBS next year and how much they would pay. The numbers were a lifeline for countless families. And this strategy, one that had never been seen before and which has never been repeated since, was intended to pump enough viewers into that tube to make CBS king once again.

Brown remained unimpressed. So I ushered him out of my office and down the hall to a conference room where two of my research executives, Jay Eliasberg and Arnie Becker, were waiting. The room was dim save for a spotlight pointing at a flip board showing the latest Nielsen figures. According to the data, we had clawed our way to the top of the ratings for the last three weeks of February. If we could maintain that streak through all of March and half of April, Becker explained, there was a chance that we might just make it. True, it meant attracting almost two and a half million viewers more than NBC in each of the 49 half-hour prime-time slots over the next six weeks. But we could do it.

Had we not proved it just a week or so earlier when we scored the third-highest TV movie ratings in history with the broadcast of *Born Free?*

I left Brown with Eliasberg and Becker and staggered back to my office. It had been a tumultuous 22 years in television. Hard to believe that the industry had changed so much since those early days when I first walked through the doors of NBC in the year that network television was born.

2.

1948 — Television's Year

"1948—TELEVISION'S YEAR… An exciting promise is now an actual service to the American home. After 20 years of preparation, the NBC television network is open for business… The greatest means of mass communications in the world is now with us." – Newspaper advertisement announcing the birth of NBC, 1948.

I very nearly never made it into television. My interview at NBC was in 1948, the year that the network formally announced its TV service and 20 years after its technicians had first begun tinkering with live broadcasts. I stood in Rockefeller Plaza, looking up at the solemn monolith of the 70-floor RCA building where the Radio Corporation of America housed its NBC division—and wondered why an entertainment company would want to hide behind such austere walls. Show business was supposed to be glamorous. So where was the massive sign—bold, flashing neon if I had had my way—telling passersby that exciting things were happening inside? As I would soon learn, though television projected an image of glamour and fun, the projectionist could often be a stuffy old man.

I had been recommended for the job by a friend, Allan Kalmus, who was director—and sole member—of NBC's fledgling television press office. My resume was not very promising.

Born in Detroit on September 11, 1921, I had a B.A. in Economics from the University of Michigan, where I had been a consistent C student. During the war I had worked as an editor for the Army News Service on *Yank* and *Stars and Stripes* in New York, where I discovered an appreciation of the city's many Italian restaurants and the girls who lived at Tudor City or the nearby Windsor Terrace apartment building. I loved New York, and after I left the Army, a friend and father figure of sorts, Ben Brady, had helped me stay in Manhattan by securing me a job as a radio scriptwriter for the *Jack Albertson Comedy Show*. I was already a bit of a prankster, with a reputation for having something of a mouth, but the pressure of filling 20 or 30 pages with jokes every week was too much. When the show was canceled a couple of years later, I jumped to the press department of the New Haven Railroad, which was terribly dull.

My career was further hampered by occasional spells of insomnia and panic attacks, and I found it hard to hold down a job. In 1948, after leaving the New Haven Railroad, I ended up washing dishes at Toots Shor's restaurant on West 51st Street. Thankfully, the Veteran's Administration referred me to a young naval psychoanalyst, Dr. Charles Fisher, a little man with a wonderful sense of humor, who worked at the Mount Sinai School of Medicine on the Upper East Side. He was an expert in the field of sleep and dreaming and a classic Freudian. Sometimes I would lie on the couch and he would not say a word. If I closed the door abruptly, he would seize upon it and keep asking, "Do you want to tell me what's wrong?" By the time I arrived at NBC, at the age of 26, I had managed to bring some of my neuroses under control.

As I walked into the cavernous lobby of the RCA building, I noticed that there still was no sign to identify NBC and the wonderful radio and television programs being made there. I rode the elevator to the fourth floor where Sid Eiges, head of NBC's press department, was waiting for me in a respectable-sized corner office. Sid was an avuncular, roly-poly man, who looked as though he might have been a teacher or a butcher if he had not ended up in television. Although NBC was a titan of broadcasting, with the most successful radio network in America, television was still so experimental that its departments were always short staffed. Everybody who was anybody wanted to be in radio.

My interview was for a position as the sole assistant to the sole television press officer. And since I already knew Alan, I hoped I had a head start. I do not remember what I said or did during the interview, but when I saw Alan at a party that night he told me the job was being offered to someone else. So the following day I called Sid Eiges from a pay phone and, in the sincerest voice possible, said: "Mr. Eiges, I just wanted to thank you for taking the time to see me. I had such a wonderful interview. I understand you couldn't accept me, but I hope that at some point in the future there will be an opening and that you will consider me again."

There was a pause, and Eiges said, "Listen, kid. Why don't you come in and we'll talk about it."

The television press job might have gone, but Eiges found me a place in the radio press department. And a couple of days later, I started work fielding calls from The New York Times and Variety about NBC's radio shows. These were the days when radio was king. And I had a wonderful time dealing with reporters, listening in on rehearsals and even talking to some of the stars. But I must have proven one of the least competent of my colleagues because in less than a year I was shunted into the no-man's land of television, which was so new that the entire department was crammed into the fourth floor of the RCA building.

Television might not have been the most desirable destination for a broadcasting employee, but it certainly was exciting. Every show went out live, and as a result we were never sure what would go wrong. In radio they only had to worry about the sound. But for television it was like staging a theater production every day of the week. In fact, we were so focused on the quality of the broadcast that content often took a backseat to the presentation itself. The success of most shows was judged not by critical acclaim, but by how well the picture and sound came out and whether the program finished on time. Each morning I would walk into the office and people would be passing comments like "the picture was so clear last night" or "the sound was marvelous." No one cared if the boom mike dropped into the picture or if the camerawork was shaky. Our viewers did not even care what program was on. The important thing was that they were watching television.

Contrary to its bland exterior, the RCA building was alive with the words and music and laughter of some of the century's greatest stars, singers, actors, musicians and comedians. Our offices were equipped with a sound system that allowed us to tune in to any studio in the building and to eavesdrop on whatever was going on. The NBC Symphony Orchestra practiced about four times a week in the enormous studio 8-H before broadcasting live each Saturday night from 6 p.m. to 7 p.m. And one of my greatest thrills was to listen in on rehearsals conducted by the director of the orchestra, the great Arturo Toscanini, who was perhaps the world's leading maestro of his day. The music was wonderful. But just as entertaining were the sections in between the music when Toscanini, who could be a petty tyrant, swore at the musicians and made fresh-sounding remarks to the female singers in Italian.

When I tired of Toscanini, I could flick a switch and tune in to studio 5-H where a Borscht Belt comic, Milton Berle, was rehearsing for his role as host of one of the first major television comedy-variety shows, *Texaco Star Theater*. Berle appeared in front of a tiny studio audience of no more than about 200 people for one hour each Tuesday night, punctuating his guests' appearances with his brash vaudeville song, dance and gag routines that consisted of rapid-fire jokes, exaggerated facial expressions and ludicrous costumes. Berle was used to working in close proximity to the raucous crowds at Catskill summer resorts and nightclubs, and the studio audience loved his brazen yet intimate style. The audience's energy and enthusiasm carried over the airwaves into people's homes, where the lucky few who had a television would often be joined by friends and neighbors crowded around their eight- or 10-inch set.

Texaco Star Theater was scheduled at 8 p.m., the perfect time to attract a mass audience as parents settled down for the evening and their children were not yet in bed. Within weeks Berle became television's first major star—"Mr. Television"—and at its peak his show had a rating of almost 90 percent. That means that 90 percent of homes with television sets—not just sets that were switched on—were tuned to "Uncle Miltie." Crowds would line the streets outside the RCA building to catch a glimpse of Milton. And New York restaurant owners, who suffered an enormous drop in customers on Tuesday nights, complained that Berle was bad for business. A ticket to *Texaco Star Theater* became one of the most sought-after seats in town. Even I had trouble getting a hold of one and would often make do by going along to 5-H a couple of days in advance and watching rehearsals from the studio steps.

Watching Milton Berle and listening to Toscanini were some of the most exciting moments of my early career as a 20-something television man. Since I lived only a few blocks from Rockefeller Center, I would often return in the evenings to watch live shows. Occasionally, my parents, Moses and Dorothy Dann, would visit from Detroit, and I would take them along to the studios to watch rehearsals and to meet the performers. I even introduced my father to one of his idols, the great radio newsman H.V. Kaltenborn. My access to the RCA building was also a great way of impressing my peers. I would invite girls to the studios to watch rehearsals. And if for some reason a show was sold out I could always invite her back to my place where, as an NBC employee, I had a 10-inch set of my own. Indeed, NBC encouraged its employees to hold viewing parties at their homes and to invite potential sponsors and ad agency men. The company even gave us a small allowance for entertaining, about $40. So, for a 27- or 28-year-old bachelor I was something of a heavy hitter with the ladies and one of the more popular guys about town.

I was also passionate about our business. The television audience may have been small but it was growing at an extraordinary rate. In 1947, about 200,00 homes had a television set. But by 1948 that number had doubled to almost 500,000. The Hollywood studios and their actors and actresses turned up their noses at television at their peril. Sure, there were many impediments to progress. Only one quarter of the country was connected via the coaxial cable that allowed us to transmit live television broadcasts; color was still highly experimental. But the buzz around television events, like the first televised World Series in 1947, and new shows like the 1948 kids' TV hit *Howdy Doody*, virtually ensured that television would soon surpass radio as the greatest means of mass communication. Meanwhile, the Radio Corporation of America, the parent company of NBC, was the market leader in all forms of broadcasting. RCA made millions of dollars from its NBC radio shows, and millions more selling wireless radio equipment and records. In many ways, NBC was like a glorified marketing division, churning out programs to persuade the American public to invest in RCA technology. And at the head of the company was a titan of the broadcasting industry and one of its earliest pioneers, General David Sarnoff.

"The General," as everybody called him, was a short, fat man with a slight Russian accent. He was the son of Russian Jewish immigrants and was rumored to have learned English by picking newspapers out of trash cans on the Lower East Side of New York. The General began his broadcasting career in 1906, at the age of 15, as a $5.50-a-week office boy for the wireless operator American Marconi. By 1912 he was station manager of the Marconi wireless station in New York that brought news of the sinking of the Titanic. And as a young Marconi manager, he urged his bosses to move into the emerging radio industry, to no avail. But when General Electric bought the company in 1919, creating the Radio Corporation of America, the General lobbied his new bosses with the same request. This time his calls were heeded, and he was promoted to commercial manager. By 1930, he had climbed to the top of the company and become RCA president.

The General was a visionary who ruled RCA from his perch on the 53rd floor of Rockefeller Center. Under his leadership, NBC's two radio networks, the Red and the Blue, were the most popular of their day. NBC began experimenting with television in 1928, and Sarnoff kept it at the forefront of the television industry with headline-grabbing experimental broadcasts like coverage of the opening of the 1939 World's Fair in New York. During the war he served in the Signal Corps, where he helped set up Radio Free Europe and was rewarded with the rank of Brigadier General, a title that he requested RCA staff address him by for the rest of his career.

Although the General was a broadcasting pioneer, he did not take much interest in programming. In fact, he positively disdained many of the shows transmitted by NBC, especially comedy, which he considered one of the lowest forms of entertainment. The General imagined himself a cultured individual, and only Arturo Toscanini and other highbrow programs satisfied his aspirations as a man of arts and letters. He also disdained material wealth. He gave minimum salaries, minimum bonuses, minimum everything to himself and his executives, though it did not stop him from having an oak-paneled office with a private barbershop and dressing room. He wanted to appear proper. And he particularly hated Hollywood, where he felt people conducted themselves in a very poor fashion. After all, beneath his social standing as president of RCA lay the child immigrant from the Lower East Side. And I think it was the desire to be accepted by his peers that often motivated him.

But even more than this desire, the General was driven by a fascination with technology. He was never happier than when he could fly down to his laboratories at Lancaster, Pennsylvania, where RCA made all sorts of products, from dishwashers and refrigerators to stoves and records. The General was an engineer. He derived pleasure not from creating radio and television programs, but from producing goods like the long-playing record or innovating as he did later by bringing realistic color to television. Once he had developed these products, he never showed much interested in marketing them. And although programming would ultimately be the best marketing tool to sell RCA television sets, he proved shortsighted when it came to major programming decisions. Indeed, his lack of vision in the entertainment industry was made glaringly obvious when, in 1948, he allowed his nemesis—and my future boss—Bill Paley of CBS to poach the biggest stars in broadcasting from NBC.

In those days, CBS radio led the ratings in news but NBC was the undisputed leader in entertainment. Listeners tuned in every day to stars like George Burns and Gracie Allen, Jack Benny and Bob Hope, as well as shows like *Amos 'n' Andy* and *Fibber McGee and Molly*. But these highly paid entertainers were being crippled by postwar income taxes of up to 90 percent. Many of NBC's stars were represented by Hollywood's biggest and most powerful talent agency, the Music Corporation of America, where Lew Wasserman was making a name for himself as the most important agent in the history of entertainment. In 1948, Wasserman and an MCA colleague, Taft Schreiber, came up with an ingenious way for their clients to sidestep the punishing income tax. They suggested their stars should turn their shows into businesses and sell them to the networks, allowing them to pay the much lower capital gains tax at 25 percent. The first MCA clients to try the scheme were Freeman Gosden and Charles Correll, the team behind NBC's hit radio show *Amos 'n' Andy*. But rather than going to NBC with the deal, Wasserman and Schreiber approached CBS and Paley. Just like that, *Amos 'n' Andy* was gone. And others were soon to follow. When the General heard that the next entertainer in Paley's sights was Jack Benny, he was horrified. Benny was the star of NBC's Sunday night comedy schedule, and the General was not going to give up his star comic without a fight. He offered Benny double whatever Paley was offering, and a bidding war ensued. But it was the General who blinked first.

In the end, the General could not rationalize paying such an inflated sum for an entertainer. He believed that the network would always be more important than the star. And he was not about to start pandering to overpaid celebrities. Besides, his legal advisor, the stuffy George T. Cahill, told him the deal was sure to be ruled illegal in the courts, and the last thing the General wanted was to become entangled in legal affairs. Above all, I think, he never imagined Benny would leave the number-one network in the country for the sake of a few extra dollars. Much later, Wasserman told New Yorker reporter Connie Bruck that the General had summoned Benny to the RCA building and told him point blank: "Nobody tunes in to Jack Benny—they tune in to NBC. We're not making this deal." And I would not be surprised if that was true.

Paley, on the other hand, knew the value of a star. During the 1940s he had fought a losing ratings battle with NBC, and had learned the hard way that the play's the thing. He needed talent like *Amos 'n' Andy* and Jack Benny if he had any hope of surpassing NBC. And legal counsel Judge Samuel Rosenman, an advisor to Roosevelt and Truman, urged him to take the deal and let the courts decide. Judge Rosenman argued that it would take at least a year for the case to make its way through the legal system, and by then Paley would already have his stars whatever they decided. As it happens, the Bureau of Internal Revenue closed the loophole before other entertainers could cash in. Nevertheless, over the coming months, MCA negotiated the transfer of a number of stars from NBC to CBS, including Edgar Bergen, Red Skelton, Groucho Marks, George Burns and Gracie Allen. Meanwhile, the fledgling American Broadcasting Company lost one of its early stars, Bing Crosby.

The exodus of celebrities went down in history as the "Paley Raids." And with his new arsenal of entertainers, Paley created a highly profitable radio business that helped pay for the ensuing and very costly experimentation in television. One of the first meetings I attended with the General at NBC was soon after Paley had poached Benny and scheduled him on CBS radio at 7 p.m. on a Sunday to great fanfare. The General wanted to show CBS that he meant business, and he asked which was our best radio show on Sunday night, the most popular listening time of the week. I piped up that it was the bandleader Horace Heidt.

"Put in Horace Heidt at seven o'clock Sunday night and we'll show them," the General ordered.

But the band leader was no match for a comedian. Benny was a ritual in the United States. His initial ratings were even higher on CBS than they had been on NBC. Meanwhile, Horace Heidt's show was canceled within a month. It was a total disaster. With such a strong lineup of performers, CBS's ratings soared. At the end of 1949, CBS radio surpassed NBC for the first time in 20 years with 12 of the top 15 shows.

But much as I cared about radio, my focus was on television, and I jumped at every chance to play a role in the ensuing programming battles with CBS. I was a compulsive worker. And as an early entrant into the industry I had the good fortune to be given free rein in all aspects of the business. Although my early jobs had specific titles—"trade editor," "coordinator of program package sales," "director of program sales"—my day-to-day responsibilities varied greatly. Television was such a new field that everybody did a little bit of everything. There was barely a dividing line between news and entertainment. And my duties included fielding public relations calls, traveling the country selling programs to sponsors, and overseeing production of shows. It was in these early days that I learned my first important lessons about the power of television as an attendance form.

At its most basic level, television transports people out of their living rooms. It gives them the best seat in the house at sporting events, plays and concerts. It is true to this day that many people would much prefer to watch in the comfort of their living room than in a stadium or a theater, dozens of feet from the attraction. Indeed, in the late 1940s sports were a major draw for the television networks. Boxing was an ideal event because it required minimal camerawork and, unlike other sports that feared television would hurt ticket sales, it had so few ringside seats that promoters were only too happy to sell the rights.

In years to come, network news would also prove to be an incredibly powerful force. But for now, NBC relied upon John Cameron Swayze, a likable former Kansas City announcer-turned-journalist who recounted the headlines on the *Camel News Caravan*. Swayze did not so much report the news as read it. And he often seemed much more interested in his ties than in the events that had occurred that day. A colleague once joked that if a President was ever to be shot, you would have to underline the word shot to make sure Swayze realized it was important. We had nothing to compare with the radio news team at CBS, led by Edward R. Murrow, a wartime friend of Paley's, and a host of other great radio newsmen like Charles Collingwood, Elmer Davis and Eric Sevareid, who would soon revolutionize TV news.

But despite the loss of NBC's stars and its second-rate news team, NBC was still the network to beat. We had been more successful for much longer than CBS. And although we suffered a few setbacks around the turn of the decade, we still had many shows to be proud of, none more so than *Philco Television Playhouse*, a live drama series that went out on the busiest hour of the busiest night in television, Sunday night at 9 p.m.

First airing in October 1948, *Philco* ran for seven years, led by one of the most talented producer-directors American television has ever seen, Fred Coe. When *Philco Playhouse* began, it relied solely on screen adaptations of plays, short stories and novels. But by the early 1950s Fred had run out of material, and he started to search for original scripts to fill the hour each week. Fred had a wonderful sense of drama and a talent for spotting scripts that would shine on television. But more than that, he was a writer's producer with a gift for recognizing and nurturing great writers. In his search for new material, Fred turned to young, mostly unknown people, who went on to become some of the greatest talents of the 20th century. Paddy Chayefsky, Gore Vidal, Tad Mosel, Horton Foote and Alan Arthur all got their start writing television plays for Fred at *Philco Playhouse*. The show, which was later sponsored by Goodyear and also known as *Goodyear Television Playhouse*, became a mecca for New York's ambitious writers, many of whom had never written for radio before, let alone television. At its height, the shows were the epitome of what came to be known as "the golden age" of television that stretched through most of the 1950s and filled the schedule with other great live anthology shows like *Kraft Television Theater* and *Studio One*, where writers like Reggie Rose, JP Miller, and Rod Serling tackled the most pressing social issues of the day.

The reliance upon original scripts every week caused huge problems at NBC, especially for Fred. Even though production usually started three weeks in advance, there was almost never enough time to rehearse properly before the show went out live, and there were often concerns that scripts might not appear at all. Final drafts usually arrived sometime on Wednesday, but rewrites and rehearsals often continued right through Sunday morning. Added to that was the logistical nightmare of getting scenery in and out of the RCA building. I loved it, living on the edge like that: the excitement, the passion of the writers and director, the actors and Fred, collaborating and arguing, laughing and crying with each other. Fred would sometimes call me at home on a Saturday morning in a complete panic, saying: "I don't know what we're going to do on Sunday night. I don't know if it's going to work." And I would calm him down and tell him everything would be okay.

Of course, there were some perfectly awful shows. But there were also some tremendous hits. Perhaps the most famous of all was Paddy Chayefsky's *Marty*, in 1953, directed by Delbert Mann and starring Rod Steiger as a lonely, young and fairly unattractive butcher from the Bronx who falls in love with a girl at a local dance. Despite its low-key storyline about an average guy and an average girl, something about *Marty* appealed to Hollywood, which turned Chayefsky's script into an Oscar- and Palme-d'Or–winning movie, again directed by Delbert Mann but this time starring Ernest Borgnine. Television, which so many people had sneered at in its early days, was suddenly attracting major talent and a great deal of attention from writers and stars. Now you could turn the television dial any night of the week and watch expertly crafted plays starring people like Grace Kelly or Eve Marie Saint, Paul Newman or Steve McQueen.

Philco and *Goodyear* continued to churn out hits for NBC for many years, including Gore Vidal's *Visit to a Small Planet*, which was made into a movie in 1960, and Horton Foote's *A Trip to Bountiful*, which became a stage play and later a movie. Fred was so proud of his stable of writers. Everybody wanted to work for him and nobody criticized him. He was a gentle family man. We would often go for walks together on the beach at Edgartown on Martha's Vineyard or in the Hamptons. Fred would talk in a soft, quiet tone about the shows he wanted to produce and the latest scripts that he was excited about. Money was not important to him; we never feared that we might lose him to CBS like some of the others—and we never did.

But you cannot build a winning schedule on one show alone. To win the ratings wars the General needed a television visionary. And fortunately for the General, his son Robert Sarnoff was friends with just such a man, Sylvester L. "Pat" Weaver Jr., vice president in charge of radio, television and movies for the advertising agency Young & Rubicam. At Y&R, Pat Weaver was in charge of nine of the top 10 prime-time shows on television. In 1949, the Sarnoffs lured Pat away from his job in advertising. And within a couple of years, an entirely new way of producing and scheduling programs was born.

3.

TV Hero

"You don't find many advertising men telling The Saturday Evening Post how to rewrite its feature articles, but hardly an advertising man is now alive who hasn't tried to be a helpful showman to some poor, broken-down, neurotic writer or producer, who only wants to do as good a job as he can—silly boy." – NBC president Sylvester L. "Pat" Weaver, Jr., "The Communicator," The New Yorker, October 23, 1954.

The National Broadcasting Company may have carried some of the greatest shows in the early years of television, but unfortunately for the General we did not own most of them. Instead, the programs were produced by our sponsors, like Colgate-Palmolive-Peet or Firestone, and their advertising agencies, such as the William Morris Agency and Young & Rubicam. All you had to do was look at the schedule to see the extent of NBC's weakness. Our most successful shows had names like *Kraft Television Theater, Texaco Star Theater, Philco* and *Goodyear Playhouse*. It was the executives of these companies who dictated the final edits of scripts, and the producers, directors and actors who would bring them to life. The sponsors sometimes even dictated the day and time their program would appear on television. It was enough to drive a programming department crazy.

The motion picture industry was never imposed upon in this way by advertisers, nor were the theater or the publishing worlds. But the simple fact was that unlike their entertainment cousins, radio and television were created primarily as a means for selling goods and services. Show business was merely a secondary concern. And despite the fact that we ran one of the most successful radio and television networks in the country, with five radio and five television stations and a network of hundreds of affiliates, we were little more than delivery boys, transmitting our sponsors' shows to their customers' homes. Almost the entire network schedule catered to the whims of the sponsor, with little regard for program order or what the competing networks were showing. At least that was the case before the General hired Pat Weaver.

Pat transformed the television industry at a rate that makes the growth of the modern cell phone look sluggish. He was like a god to me; tall, lean as a pin, well educated and sophisticated. The son of a California millionaire, he schooled at Dartmouth, where he roomed with Nelson Rockefeller (whom Pat always referred to as "Rags"). Pat was about a foot taller than me—6 foot 4 inches—and taller still when wobbling on top of a wooden contraption called a Bongo Board to practice for the frequent skiing vacations he took with his wife, Liz. I often thought that to the three secretaries stationed outside his sixth-floor corner office we must have looked like Mutt and Jeff. From atop the Bongo Board, or when seated behind his enormous L-shaped desk, Pat would expound upon his ideas for taking control of programming away from the sponsor and for making television a truly democratizing and enlightening medium.

It might be difficult to imagine today, but in the 1950s Pat really thought that television could improve the lot of the common man; that we at NBC could enlighten a nation through our programming and that the only thing standing in our way, apart from technological constraints and budgets, was the advertiser, who cared only about reaching the largest number of homes at the lowest possible cost. About this subject Pat knew more than most. Before arriving at NBC he had been a vice president of Young & Rubicam in charge of radio, television and movies, and before that advertising director of American Tobacco. When Pat worked on the sponsor side of the industry, he fought vigorously for advertiser control of programming. But now that he was an NBC man, he fought just as vigorously for the network to reassert its authority and to develop experimental, big-budget programming that would educate the viewer on such a grand scale and at such enormous cost that no one sponsor could afford to exert total control. Over the course of the next few years we would introduce what became known as "the long form"—shows which ran for 90 minutes to two-and-a-half hours and which made the budget for *Philco Play-house* seem like pocket change.

Pat's overriding concern was to educate the American public, not just through news and current affairs, but also through entertainment. He launched initiatives with names like "Operation Wisdom" and "Operation Frontal Lobes" to bring a more cerebral form of programming to the airwaves. As part of his drive to ensure NBC's schedule was as educational as possible, he instructed producers to submit weekly "responsibility reports" detailing how they had enlightened or enriched the viewing public, whether the show was *Robert Mont-gomery Presents* or *Howdy Doody*. I was assigned to enforce the reporting process and to inform Pat of any lapses in content. Bettering the American people became a weekly, daily, hourly goal.

Pat delivered rousing speeches and dictated erudite memos—many of which I still have today—underlining the importance of this one simple, yet elusive, ambition. His memos, which often ran to dozens of pages and became the stuff of legend within the industry, would glide across the centuries and the arts, crisscrossing multiple disciplines, from ancient Greece to Tuesday night comedy, from Albert Einstein to Arthur Godfrey. Pat had been a brilliant scholar of classics and philosophy at Dartmouth. And to stimulate his subordinates he would send us home with some light reading, like the complete works of Albert Schweitzer. He often communicated in long, philosophical phrases that were totally new to the television world. This, for example, is an interdepartmental memo from February 1955, in which Pat reminds staff of a letter he addressed to the programming department three years earlier calling on NBC to help television achieve its potential as "the most vital force for cultural good since speech itself."

> *"The letter pointed out that we would, of course, always do separate public affairs, news, and informational programs. But that the chance to enlighten, illuminate, inform the maximum number of people exists in the shows of the schedule that reach all families and all members of all families. So, the instruction was for the insertion and conscious integration of informational and cultural matter in existing shows. This was intended to enable us to do what old-time radio broadcasting failed to do—to air inspiring kinds of segment programming at all times of the day and night, all over the schedule (including prime nighttime periods), and to larger numbers of people than ever reached by any medium in history."*

This was Weaver-speak at its best. And as well as being Pat's arms and legs, it fell to me to be his interpreter. It was often my job to explain what Pat had just written or said to a team of befuddled executives and producers who were more concerned with how they were actually going to put a show on the air than with educating the great American masses. But the technicalities of program production were of no concern to Pat, who was fixated on elevating the content of shows so that television would become more than what he disparagingly referred to as the "jukebox in the living room." Pat's one overriding concern was that NBC should improve the life and knowledge of the average American. And on the following page of that 1955 memo, underlined, was a typical Weaver command:

It is not enough that the American people shall be superbly entertained. They must be kept informed. It is your job, nobody else's, because you have the circulation at your command. Responsibility must be kept alive—and I know you have the individual conscience and the wish to meet the obligation.

Apart from his desire to raise the quality of broadcasting, there were other reasons why Pat wanted to take control of production away from the sponsors, not least of which was their constant meddling in shows. Throughout the early days of television, companies took extreme caution in case the content of programs damaged their image or offended potential customers. Therefore, the poor scriptwriter who dreamt up a storyline involving an accidental fire in a show sponsored by a tobacco manufacturer would be sent scurrying back to his typewriter. Chevrolet once removed the phrase "fording a stream" from a show because it mentioned one of their competitors. Even "golden age" shows, like the award-winning *Kraft Television Theater*, suffered under the watchful eye of their sponsor. During its 11-year run, *Kraft*, produced by the J. Walter Thompson agency, stuck almost exclusively to storylines that explored safe, middle-class suburban values—because the entire reason for the show was to sell food to middle-class suburban housewives. Meanwhile, over at *Studio One* on CBS, Reggie Rose was forced to change the protagonist of one of his greatest television plays, *Thunder on Sycamore Street*, from an African-American into an ex-convict, because sponsors feared it would put off customers in the South.

The meddling only intensified during McCarthyism, when the blacklists that had engulfed Hollywood's movie industry spilled over into television. In June 1950, a group calling itself *Counterattack* published *Red Channels*, a booklet naming and shaming 151 members of the entertainment profession, including the actor Lee J. Cobb, the TV writer Nat Hiken, and the singer Pete Seeger. At first *Red Channels* had little impact. But as the hysteria grew, and as the affiliates started to get complaints from angry, letter-writing viewers, *Red Channels* began to exert a powerful influence over the industry. It permeated the profession like a poison gas, never outwardly cited as a reason for hiring or firing an actor or a scriptwriter, but always lurking in the atmosphere.

I can still remember the day clearly, a Sunday in August 1950, two months after it was published, when the controversy overwhelmed me. I was sitting at my desk in NBC's press department when I got a call from an executive at General Foods. The firm was concerned that the actress Jean Muir, who was about to debut in the second season of the General Foods–sponsored comedy show *The Aldrich Family*, was among the list of names in *Red Channels*. Muir denied being a Communist, but General Foods said it did not matter, the association was bad enough. And both the company and its advertising agency, Young & Rubicam, demanded that she be thrown off the show immediately. As it happened, Jean was married to a friend of mine, a lawyer named Henry Jaffe. And I had to spend the next 24 hours firing off press releases explaining NBC's decision to drop Muir and postpone the show until a suitable replacement could be found. It was one of the saddest days of my early career, and I told Jean and Henry repeatedly that I was sorry there was nothing more I could do. Jean could not get another job in television for almost 10 years.

Far less serious, but just as frustrating for NBC, was the frivolous meddling that many company executives felt entitled to since they were the ones putting up the money for the shows. In September 1950, Pat brought *The Comedy Hour*, a Sunday night prime-time show, to the nation's screens in direct competition with Ed Sullivan's ratings-topping *Toast of the Town* on CBS. *The Comedy Hour* had an enormous budget and a rotating cast of big-name hosts that, in its first year, included Bob Hope, Eddie Cantor, Fred Allen, Dean Martin and Jerry Lewis. The show was sponsored on alternate weeks by Colgate and Frigidaire and was known as *The Colgate Comedy Hour* and *The Frigidaire Comedy Hour*, depending upon which company was underwriting the show. Within a matter of weeks, it displaced *Toast of the Town* for the number-one spot in the ratings. Nevertheless, Pat faced untold problems with the sponsors, particularly the chief executive of Colgate-Palmolive-Peet, Edward Little.

Pat had no time for authority, title and rank. And no patience for arrogant executives who thought they knew something about television. He held comedians in the highest esteem, possibly because his brother was a second-rate comic called Doodles Weaver. But for interfering sponsors he had only contempt. He gave Edward Little the nickname "Swamp Fox" because of his predatory nature and two beady eyes that seemed to swivel high on his face. Pat was normally so mild-mannered and charming. Yet he would go rigid at the mere mention of the Swamp Fox's name. Whenever Little stopped by the RCA building, Pat would call me into his office to listen as the Swamp Fox dictated how "his show" ought to be run. He would critique the last week's performance and lend his advice on which compères and guests had failed to live up to expectations. To this day I do not know how, but before long Little forced Frigidaire out of the picture and Colgate became the sole sponsor of the program.

The annual budget for the *Colgate Comedy Hour* ran to millions of dollars, giving Little an exceedingly strong bargaining position. When the show opened in the second season with Jackie Gleason hosting for the first time, Little told Pat point blank, "I don't want that fat man on my show anymore." That was the end of Gleason's *Comedy Hour* career. When Pat suggested replacing Gleason with a talented comedian by the name of Phil Silvers, Little vetoed that idea too. And this was not for just any old show. This was for our top-rated show at 8 p.m. Sunday, the busiest television night of the week. Something had to be done to prevent the Swamp Foxes of the world from killing television.

Pat's solution was simple: Make shows so big and so expensive that they would be beyond the budget of even the most powerful advertiser, bring production of the show in-house, and then carve the program into advertising segments, selling slots to a number of different sponsors. For his inspiration, Pat looked to magazines, which sold different-sized advertising spaces to a range of companies across a number of pages. Before long, the "magazine format" was being employed to finance a number of highly successful NBC shows.

Pat's first great success in this form was a two-and-a-half hour weekly variety show called *Saturday Night Revue*. The program was split into two sections. The first hour, broadcast from Chicago, was a vaudeville production called *The Jack Carter Show*. And the second hour and a half, broadcast from New York, was a comedy-variety show called *Your Show of Shows*. The entire program cost about $50,000 a week and was far too big for any one sponsor to finance, so Pat chopped the program into half-hour chunks and sold three minutes of ad time per 30-minute segment. Sponsors and their agencies balked at the idea of sharing space with a competitor in a single program. And they were indignant that they could no longer associate their product, and their product alone, with a single program. For its opening week in February 1950, we failed to sell a single one of the 15 advertising slots.

But what the sponsors had not reckoned upon, and what Pat knew only too well, was that if the show was a success there would be a stampede of advertisers eager to put their name to *Saturday Night Revue*, even if some of the haughtier firms felt it was beneath them. *The Jack Carter Show* was a decent enough program. But *Your Show of Shows*, produced by Max Liebman and starring Sid Caesar, Imogene Coca, Carl Reiner and Howard Morris, was a smash. And it was no wonder, considering that the talent in front of the cameras was mirrored by a backroom staff that included such wonderful writers as Mel Tolkin, Lucille Kallen, Mel Brooks and later Neil Simon and Woody Allen.

Every week for 39 weeks, the writers had to come up with four or five new comedy sketches as well as the *gazintas*, the witty monologues that introduced whichever acts Max had booked for that week. (The reason they called them *gazintas*, Max told me, was because "this act *gazinta* that one.") Max was a real lover of classical arts, so each week it was not unusual to see the Billy Williams Quartet or the Hamilton Trio followed by the soprano Marguerite Piazza or an excerpt from a ballet. Meanwhile, in the cramped writer's room at West 56th Street—made famous by Neil Simon's *Laughter on the 23rd Floor*—the atmosphere was intense as Tolkin and his team threw lines across the room, ridiculing and refining each other's ideas. They were young and brash and unafraid of stepping out of line. I remember Carl telling me how once he and Mel Brooks were walking down 57th Street, approaching Carnegie Hall, when they saw a couple of nuns walking towards them. Carl knew that Mel could not let two nuns pass unremarked and sure enough, no sooner were they level than Mel walked right up to them and started barking like a director: "All right, sisters. The sketch is canceled. Get back to wardrobe and get those clothes off!" And then just kept right on walking.

Those writers worked under such strain, having to come up with material week in and week out. But despite their irreverence and the show's huge success, we never had any trouble with the stars or the writers. In fact, I was the only one who caused trouble because however good the talent was, as the weeks and seasons went on our ratings began to decline and I started badgering Max to do something to improve the numbers. By the third season I had pretty much had enough and I called Max into my office and told him, "Look, Max, it's always the same thing—first Marguerite Pizza, second The Hamilton Trio, third the Billy Williams Quartet, and fourth Marge and Gower Champion. The numbers are down. You've got to give it a new look."

"Mike," Max said. "Don't worry about it. I'll take care of it. You watch next week."

The next week came, and once again it was the same performers doing the same shtick. I called Max at home and said, "Max, you did the same goddamned show. You promised me."

"What are you talking about?" Max said, sounding hurt. "You didn't notice it? This week the Billy Williams Quartet went on second and the Hamilton Trio went on third."

Saturday Night Revue was a big hit. But more importantly it laid the groundwork for one of Pat's greatest legacies: the *Today* show. Pat had been trying to convince the General and NBC's advertisers about his idea for an early morning show since the turn of the decade. In the early 1950s, most television stations did not go on the air until about 10 a.m., and real programming did not get going until the late afternoon. Conventional wisdom held that people did not watch television in the morning, which was dominated by radio.

I first learned of *Today* in 1951 when Pat asked me to help him build a dedicated staff for a new program and handed me a memo laying out his plans for a two-hour morning show. My gut instinct was that it would never work, and I told him so straight away. Who was going to look at TV first thing in the morning with all the radio programs on and with people getting ready to go to work? But Pat told me to finish the memo. And by the time I reached the end I was convinced it was a brilliant idea.

Pat had an entire thesis behind the *Today* show. His argument was that while the American people were asleep in bed, things were happening around the world that they needed to know about as soon as they woke up. He reasoned that since three quarters of homes used the radio between 7 a.m. and 9 a.m., why not television? The show was to be a symbol of television's ability to bring the latest news straight into the home. But it would not just be a sober current affairs show. It would be a mishmash of news and music, weather and traffic updates, interviews with writers and actors. Although the show would be visual, it would be light enough and concentrate sufficiently on the spoken word so that the audience would not need to pay attention as they moved about the house getting dressed and eating their breakfast. And right there in the memo was a bold idea to bring the show instant attention: Pat wanted to commandeer the RCA showroom at 49th Street in Times Square and turn it into a glass-fronted television studio from which he could broadcast the show directly into the street through loudspeakers and where passersby could look in as the show was transmitted around the nation. Naturally, the General was cautious about such a piece of blatant showmanship, not to mention giving up his beloved showroom for a television program. But Pat told him the *Today* show was of greater importance than selling a few RCA products in New York. Besides, if it was a success, it would do more to sell RCA television sets across the country than a single showroom in Times Square.

The General acquiesced. And no sooner did we have his approval than Pat set about planning a studio that would symbolize the technological expertise behind, and international scope of, his program. We filled the showroom with every instrument we could find that epitomized communications wizardry: teletype machines, telephones, TV monitors, weather maps and, of course, a battery of clocks showing time zones around the world. While the showroom was an inspired piece of public relations, it also presented one major concern: that the noise from the people and the traffic outside, particularly the sirens of passing emergency vehicles, would distract from the program. Little did we know that the dynamics of New York City life, and the gawkers looking through the window, would transport people in Omaha, Nebraska—or wherever they were in America—to the heart of the Big Apple.

The *Today* staff worked hard. They were up by 5 a.m. each morning, in rehearsals by 6 a.m. and on air from 7 a.m. until 9 a.m. My job was to supervise the show; being there on the day of the first broadcast in January 1952 was one of the greatest thrills of my life. I had suggested an announcer, Ernie Kovacs, to be the presenter of *Today*. At the time, Kovacs was already working on the only early-morning show on U.S. television, a locally produced program called *Three to Get Ready*, which aired on our Philadelphia affiliate WPTZ. But Pat wanted Dave Garroway, an easygoing and somewhat unconventional former announcer from Chicago, who had just finished an immensely popular musical-variety show, *Garroway at Large*. Pat also chose Mort Werner as the producer. Garroway and Werner were well suited to the task and easily gifted enough to create a successful show. But initial viewing figures were poor and the critics were less than charitable. Writing in The New York Herald Tribune, John Crosby called *Today* "a two-hour comedy of errors."

True, there were some initial technical glitches, and we did overreach at the outset with a sometimes confusing array of features, including weather reports that were called in via telephone from Europe. We were also hampered by our affiliates, only half of whom opened their stations early enough to carry the show, and by sponsors who remained skeptical that viewers would tune in so early in the morning. The first edition of *Today*, which cost about $40,000 to produce, had just one sponsor. But gradually the program changed. It became less and less about bringing people up to date with events around world and more a folksy show with friendly people that discussed national news and social issues. Over the coming months viewing figures began to climb steadily as did interest from sponsors. One of the most exciting events was when, in a single commercial break, we carried messages from both General Motors and the Appian Way pizza pie company. I also remember persuading a poor newscaster to demonstrate a Bissell Carpet Sweeper by rolling it backwards and forwards over the studio floor in between news reports. Within three or four months, *Today* was paying for itself. But it was not the sponsors or the affiliates, the technological expertise or the Times Square showroom, Dave Garroway or even Pat Weaver, that guaranteed that the *Today* show became a part of America's breakfast. That honor goes to a chimpanzee called J. Fred Muggs.

I do not remember why J. Fred Muggs first appeared on *Today*. But I do remember that he was an instant hit, especially with the kids who called all their friends to see the chimp on the show and who talked about it at school. Thousands of children forced their parents to turn the television set on in the mornings. The ratings shot up, and advertisers fell over each other in the rush to sponsor the show. We could not believe the excitement J. Fred Muggs had generated. He became an institution and as important as everyone else on the show. He would sit on Dave Garroway's knee during interviews and jump around during skits. By the end of the 1952 season, *Today* was lauded as the biggest-grossing show of the year, out-earning *Gone with the Wind*. The chimpanzee was probably one of the greatest stimuli to a program's ratings in TV history.

For Dave Garroway, being upstaged by a chimpanzee was a cruel twist, especially as he was the one who had to put up with J. Fred Muggs acting up most mornings, including attacking colleagues and urinating around the studio. One day, a stern-looking Garroway strode into my office. "Mike, you know, we work pretty hard on that show. It's a serious show. And that chimpanzee is running around here grabbing the papers, pissing on people, pulling their hair and distracting me when I'm working. And I can't take it any more. You have to get rid of it. In fact, if you don't get rid of it, I'm quitting."

What could I do? People loved the chimp. He doubled our ratings. "Dave," I said. "You're a wonderful presenter. Please don't force me to make that decision."

Garroway walked out in a huff. But he stayed on the show and so did the chimp. The fact of the matter was that I could easily have found another Dave Garroway, but it would have been much harder to find another J. Fred Muggs. If I had lost him I would have lost half my audience. And as I was quickly learning, in television it did not matter who or what was on the screen; as long as the audience came, you could always find someone to sponsor the show.

4.

Spectaculars!

"When our artists, writers and producers learn the use of the new form, we will vastly enrich the television schedule. And if we do not enrich and vitalize our programming, the ever-present danger threatening all mass media awaits us. That is the danger of playing only to the heavy users of the medium, and getting large audiences but the same audiences… and leaving unattracted a large segment of the population which does not find the normal product sufficiently rewarding, except occasionally. The Spectacular is aimed at bringing these light users or viewers into television and making it more useful and enjoyable to them—and increasing total circulation of the network."
– Pat Weaver, "Definition of the Spectacular—as a show form and as an advertising form," memo to NBC programming staff, January 1955.

It should have been one of my greatest moments. In March 1955, millions of families gathered around their television sets and those of friends and neighbors to watch Mary Martin and Cyril Ritchard in the screen adaptation of the smash Broadway musical *Peter Pan*. The broadcast was the first time such a production had been transplanted from the stage to television, and the evening could not have gone better. Mary was superb, the costumes looked wonderful broadcast in color and, best of all, the flying technology we had imported from England, and which I had been so worried might malfunction on the night, worked without a hitch. All told, the production was easily worth the $700,000 or so price tag—later vindicated by the estimated 70 million Americans who tuned in that night.

I was standing in the wings, and as the production came to a close I began playing over in my mind the modest response I would give to the General's and Pat's praise.

"Why thank you, General, but I had very little do with it," I imagined myself saying deferentially. "It's Clark"—Clark Jones, our director—"and his team who deserve all the credit, really."

Lost in my reverie it took a few moments before I noticed that despite the production having come to a close, the audience appeared to be cheering and applauding as though something was still entertaining them on stage. I peered out and, to my horror, saw our star Mary Martin ad-libbing a flying routine 20 feet or so above the audience. First she zoomed one way, then she zoomed the other. Gracefully, joyfully, hurtling backwards and forwards over the delighted crowd as the credits rolled across America. I had visions of her swinging off the wire—and disappearing off screen—being injured or killed in front of one-third of America. Live. On television. Every ounce of self-satisfaction drained from my body as I stood for 30 seconds, 60 seconds, 90 seconds—why the hell did they have to acknowledge so many people?—until eventually the credits stopped rolling and Mary landed backstage. As the stagehands unhooked her, I walked over, trembling, and politely asked, "Mary, what were you doing out there? That wasn't in the script was it?"

"No, Mike," she said, panting and exhilarated. "But don't you think it made the credits a little more interesting?"

Of course, she was right. It was in the spirit of the production. And it capped a phenomenal performance that Jack Gould of The New York Times called "an unforgettable evening of video theater," ending his glowing review with the plea that it would not be the last "of the Broadway productions that... will decide to 'go on tour' via coast-to-coast television." But live television was such a scary experience in those days that the last thing I needed was a star improvising the end of a show 20 feet above the audience.

Peter Pan was one of dozens of NBC "spectaculars" that I helped oversee during the 1950s. Once again, Pat was the driving force behind these one-off shows—which nowadays are referred to as "specials"—that were inserted into the schedule to shake up programming. Looking back, it seems remarkable that we managed to produce so many one-off shows, starring some of the biggest names in movies. Imagine today if every couple of weeks, NBC presented an original 90-minute show, starring Brad Pitt or Angelina Jolie or Will Smith or Nicole Kidman. Because that is pretty much what Pat set out to do. The idea behind spectaculars was that a single, big-budget event, headlined by the biggest stars, would make television exciting and would dramatically increase ratings.

But there was a second motive too: color. RCA and CBS had been competing for years over color technology. Both companies had found different solutions to the problem of how to transmit a color picture to the television home. And in 1953, RCA won the battle when the Federal Communications Commission (FCC) adopted RCA color as the American standard. People could watch color broadcasts on black-and-white sets. But one of the ideas behind spectaculars was to convince Americans to go out and invest in color TV. At NBC, word came down from the General that we were to come up with new programming ideas that would help sell RCA color televisions. In the first few months of 1954 every NBC show was broadcast in color at least once. The spectaculars were an additional, not to mention exceptional, color sales pitch.

Pat's thesis for the spectacular was that we could not only push color, but also attract a whole new portion of the audience for whom television was not yet an essential part of life. Needless to say, advertisers hated the concept of interrupting regularly scheduled programming for one-off shows. But following the success of the magazine format and programs such as *Saturday Night Revue* and *Today*, Pat was proving more than a match for sponsors. His ideas worked. He was bringing in money. He was building an audience.

The idea of spectaculars was not exactly new. In 1953, the Ford Motor Company had bought prime-time space across all the networks and broadcast a 50th anniversary spectacular, headlined by stars such as Marian Anderson, Mary Martin and Ethel Merman. What was special about Pat's idea was that NBC would incorporate spectaculars into the program schedule, interrupting the monotony of Saturday, Sunday and Monday night television every four weeks with a one-off, 90-minute show. For our Saturday and Sunday spectaculars we brought in Max Liebman, who had been so successful with *Your Show of Shows*, calling the program, somewhat unimaginatively, *Max Liebman Presents*. For the Monday night spectaculars, which were to be our flagship shows, we employed the producer of the Ford anniversary special, Leland Hayward.

Leland, who started out as a reporter and then a press agent, was by then one of the most colorful figures in entertainment. He was larger than life—"Mr. Broadway." We would meet every Monday at the Colony restaurant on East 61st Street. It was the society restaurant of its day, like '21' or The Four Seasons. Sinatra might be there, or Capote or Onassis. Leland would hold court with a bottle of the strongest bourbon possible, Wild Turkey I think, on the table. He was a great talker. Everybody who came in would recognize him and come over to say hello. And he in turn would be gracious and warm.

Our idea was for Leland to produce spectaculars that would both showcase RCA color technology and that would also play to television's strength as an attendance form, transporting people at home to the heart of New York City's theater district. Leland's theatrical intuition did not let us down. He dreamt up wonderful ideas, adaptations of Broadway shows and plays that would flabbergast audiences. I was incredibly excited. But a few months before *Producers' Showcase* was set to go on the air Leland suffered a heart attack. He survived, but he asked to be released from his contract.

We still had Leland's ideas for the first few shows, but no one to produce them. Then someone came up with a solution. We could bring in a rotating team of producers, shift the apostrophe in the title and call the spectaculars *Producers' Showcase*. As an insurance policy, we drafted Fred Coe, the one producer of the day who could match Leland's talent and flair, to oversee the show.

The first *Producers' Showcase* stuck to Leland's original ideas, an abridged version of Noel Coward's *Tonight at 8:30*. Coward's work comprised 10 plays in one, so we selected three, which were duly arranged for television by F. Hugh Hubert. The show starred Ginger Rogers, Trevor Howard, Gig Young and Gloria Vanderbilt, and was produced by Fred and directed by Otto Preminger. With such a talented team we thought *Tonight at 8:30* could not possibly fail. But it did. Leland had envisioned Mary Martin as the star of the show, but after Mary turned the role down we brought in Rogers, who was a major star but not the most versatile of actresses. The lead role in *Tonight at 8:30* required her to play a range of characters, from a vaudeville star to a middle-aged woman struggling to recapture her youth. And Jack Gould savaged the production in The New York Times, accusing Rogers of delivering her lines "listlessly." He described the set as "forced and unsophisticated," the direction as "static," the lighting as "uncomplimentary" and, to cap it all, he finished by saying, "the color, incidentally, was far below NBC's usually high standard." The General was not amused.

The spectaculars were very expensive, generally about $500,000 a show, and very difficult to produce—90 minutes of live, filmed entertainment. When they were good they were wonderful. But when they were bad, they were very costly failures. And since these were one-off, live performances, there were bound to be problems. Over time, we learned from our mistakes. During the second *Producers' Showcase*, an adaptation of the Pulitzer-Prize–winning Broadway comedy *State of the Union*, the actors got in the way of the cameras and the camerawork itself was a little jerky. But overall the production was a big success. *State of the Union* was the first political play shown on television, adapted from the 1945 Broadway play by its creators, Howard Lindsay and Russel Crouse. We had a top director in Arthur Penn, and Margaret Sullavan turned in a phenomenal performance. Gould called it an "almost unheard of thing to have been heard on TV" and a "viewer's minor miracle," noting that "there was a play with something provocative to say, the playwrights to say it amusingly, the players to act it and, rarest of all in video, the time to do it."

And when Gould said something like that it really meant something. We lived and died by his words. He was more than just a critic. He was like the conscience of the industry. He would examine a show with one eye on the production and another eye on the broad sweep of television. He had a terrible responsibility because to be a critic of television meant that, unlike the music critic or the theater critic, he had to be a critic of all things, from ballet to drama, from comedy to news. When Gould wrote about your show, everybody paid attention to it.

A couple of months later we presented *Yellow Jack*, the screen adaptation of Sidney Howard's play about the quest to find a cure for yellow fever. Until then, we had always chosen productions that allowed a few stars to shine, but *Yellow Jack* required a large cast and lacked the enticement of a single leading role for a major Hollywood star. So I said to Fred, "Forget about getting one or two huge names. We'll put together an entire cast of good names, not necessarily the biggest stars, but an ensemble of real quality. Everyone has to be recognizable."

Fred came back with a list bursting with talent: E.G. Marshall and Eva Marie Saint, Raymond Massey and Rod Steiger, Jackie Cooper and Wally Cox, Broderick Crawford and Dennis O'Keefe. Although Massey and Crawford had both been popular character actors for many years in Hollywood, none of the cast were what you might call top earners. They were a raft of good to great actors rather than a couple of huge stars. Gould loved the production, calling it "truly noteworthy for its gallery of individual portrayals by as fine a cast as has been gathered on one television screen this season." It proved that if you could not get a couple of really big stars, then an ensemble of decent actors added up to the same. Over the coming years if people were putting together a production and they could not get a couple of big names, they would say, "Let's Yellow Jack it."

But *Producers' Showcase* seldom had trouble attracting big names. It was one of the few places in television where major stars could shine for a full hour and a half in some of the greatest plays of the 20th century. And perhaps nothing personified the ambition of the show more than our May 1955 production of *The Petrified Forest*, directed by Delbert Mann and starring Henry Fonda, Lauren Bacall, Humphrey Bogart and Jack Klugman. It was just unbelievable to have such a cast assembled, and the show was very well received. You could not get near the studio with all those stars there, and it created such excitement in television. But the demands of live television, especially with the added obstacle of showcasing color, continued to present their own difficulties.

Hollywood actors found the rigors of live production strenuous, and rehearsals often continued right up until the very last minute. Plus, we had the technical problem of broadcasting simultaneously to a color and a black-and-white audience. The doctors in *Yellow Jack* had to wear light blue lab coats because it showed up better on black-and-white sets, which in 1955 was still the TV of choice for the majority of our audience. While this was a minor distraction for our few color viewers, the actual broadcast still came out a rather poor quality for those watching in black and white, leaving Gould to ask whether it was time the FCC stepped in "to see how compatible color and black and white TV really are."

There was also the problem of finding new and exciting productions to stage each month. It was one thing to try to inject a bit of culture into the television schedule. But to come up with a fresh project every few weeks was almost impossible. It was around this time that I was reading the newspaper one day when I saw that the ballet company from Sadler's Wells Theater in England was bringing the great ballerina Margot Fonteyn to America. The manager of her tour was the impresario Sol Hurok, so I called Hurok and asked if he would speak with me about the possibility of putting Fonteyn on U.S. television. Hurok was undoubtedly the greatest impresario of his day, possibly of all time. His roster of talent included Marian Anderson, Vladimir Ashkenazy, Sviatoslav Richter, Isadora Duncan and Andrés Segovia. Over the coming decades I would put almost all of these stars on television. But for now, our first meeting, he suggested that we meet for lunch at Le Pavillon.

Though I am more of a gourmand than a gourmet, I can safely say that Le Pavillon is one of the finest French restaurants I have ever had the privilege to patronize. The restaurant began life at the 1939 World's Fair in Queens before it was transferred by its often tyrannical owner, Henri Soulé, to East 55th Street opposite the St. Regis Hotel. It was such an elegant restaurant, the father of all the great New York French restaurants, and undoubtedly one of the first dining places where people went not just for the food, which was the apogee of haute cuisine, but also to be seen. Soulé refused to admit women in pants. He would say, "The women with the pajamas, they can't come in." And he always reserved the front of the restaurant for his best clients, stuffing the undesirables and wannabes, even his landlord Henry Cohn, in a room at the back.

Sol Hurok always sat at the front. Salvador Dali might be in the corner, and at the next table might be the Duchess of Windsor or perhaps Ambassador Kennedy. Meanwhile, Soulé would act as maître d', dressed in an impeccable blue suit, showing people to their table and meeting and greeting New York's elite. Needless to say, he did not look too happy when a 34-year-old putz from NBC arrived that lunchtime in 1955, but when I told him I was meeting Mr. Hurok, he softened slightly and showed me to the table.

I was so nervous that I do not know how many celebrities I walked past to get to Hurok, but no sooner had I sat down than I started in with my pitch.

"You know, Mr. Hurok, we're very anxious to have the great lady Margot Fonteyn dancing Sleeping Beauty with the Sadler's Wells Ballet... we have a very deep commitment to showcasing only the highest form of arts... it's very important for us to have her on the air... we could do the show for about $150,000 above the line..."

"Wait a minute," Hurok said, with a thick, Russian accent. "You're not staying for lunch?"

"Why yes, Mr. Hurok. I just thought that..."

"Well, let's have a little something to eat then. We'll have dessert, a little bit of coffee, and then, since you're staying for the food, we can talk afterwards."

It was a most elegant slap in the face. On the table in front of us were two shot glasses full of vodka, and Sol motioned to Henri Soulé who attended our table carrying a huge tin containing the finest Beluga caviar. Now, I am from Detroit. My father was a scrap metal dealer, for chrissake. He never taught me that caviar could be black. Or how to eat it.

Soulé handed me the spoon and, almost sneering, held the tin out in front of me. I had no idea how one serves caviar. I looked at Sol, who just nodded for me to proceed. So I stood slightly and, leaning forwards, prayed, "Please, God, just don't let it fall off the spoon."

As I reached towards the caviar my motion was halted by a shriek from Sol.

"Not from the side!" he screamed. "It's salty!"

In life there are moments when everything occurs in slow motion. Le Pavillon's front room was not large. And everyone—New York's most prominent personalities—was looking at me. I moved the spoon to the center of the tin, trying to ignore the stares, my face burning, took a modest scoop, dropped the caviar onto my plate, and sat down.

"My God, kid!" Sol said.

After that we became such good friends. Sol taught me that business and lunch only mix when one follows the other and that they should never be attempted at the same time. More importantly he taught me that the best time to discuss contracts and money is at the end of a meal, when your companion's resolve has been softened by food and wine, as was mine that day when we

agreed on a very generous package to bring the Sadler's Wells Ballet to *Producers'*
Showcase that December.

Moreover, Sol was just a great guy to be around. He was the very essence of
an impresario, a man of such elegance and refinement, often dressed in a top
hat and cape. He had a beautiful apartment filled with rare icons that he had
brought back from Russia, and two servants. Wherever we ate, people like the
doyenne of New York society Brooke Astor or Mrs. Irving Berlin would come
over to greet him. And for his part Sol would be so charming. Dinner parties
at his home were always attended by the greatest performers of the day, mostly
men, who would sit around the table discussing which city they were visiting
soon, usually followed by a comment about which young lady they would meet
there. They seemed like the playboys of the Western world, with a girl in every
town, though they never mentioned names in front of me.

"You were in Cleveland?"

"Yes, I was in Cleveland."

"Did you see?"

"Yeah."

"And how was she?"

"Marvelous. Simply marvelous."

Or "You're going to L.A.?"

"Next month."

"You'll see?"

"Sure."

"Give her my best."

I consider myself extremely lucky to have had a friendship with such a man.

With contacts such as Sol and a growing Rolodex of agents, *Producers'*
Showcase scored a number of critically acclaimed hits for NBC. Meanwhile,
Max Liebman Presents, which ran concurrently, was not quite as successful.
Max's first show, a musical called *Satins and Spurs*, starring Betty Hutton, was a
$300,000 disaster. Nothing worked, not the music, not the script, and certainly
not Hutton, who Max referred to as more difficult than the prima donna ice
skater Sonja Henie.

Max was used to dealing with Catskills performers like Caesar, Coca and the
Hamilton Trio. He did not know how to handle temperamental Hollywood
stars while juggling an enormous budget and the demands of live television.
Not only was the Hutton production a flop, but the next handful of shows
were poor too. Somehow Max never seemed to notice the terrible ratings or the
caustic reviews.

At the end of one particularly bad show I called Max at home. He picked up the phone, his voice sounding hopeful, and asked, "Well, Mike, what did you think?"

"Max," I replied. "You've done it again."

"It's Mike on the phone," I heard Max telling his wife, Sonia. "You won't believe what he said.

"Here, Mike, tell Sonia what you just told me," he said, handing Sonia the phone.

"Max did it again!" I told Sonia.

"Oh, thank you, Mike," Sonia said.

The Liebmans thanked me after every one of those phone calls.

But even Max was not without his successes. In December 1954, he produced a musical version of *Babes in Toyland* starring "fat" Jack Leonard. Jack Gould hated it, criticizing the casting, the humor, the staging and the picture quality. But the numbers went through the roof. The following day I got a call from our sponsor Oldsmobile. It was their top dog, Jack Wolfram, congratulating me on the production and saying how proud he was to support our show. And there was the rub. It did not matter what Jack Gould or any of the critics said; as long as the numbers were good and the sponsor was happy, so was I.

5.

When the Show Must Go On

"You can't pay the people not to come." – Samuel Goldwyn.

There is no magic formula for a successful television program. Throughout my career I have seen terrible shows that ran for years and wonderful shows that never made it to the end of the first season. A program's success can be dependent upon a single star, like Lucille Ball or Milton Berle, or on the chance convergence of a comedy writing team like Mel Tolkin, Woody Allen, Mel Brooks and Carl Reiner. As a program executive, I could do little to persuade millions of people to tune in to a show I liked, just as there was little I could do to persuade people not to tune in to a show I did not like. Samuel Goldwyn once told me: "You can't pay the people not to come." And he was right. I have promoted some of the best shows in the world, and they were never sampled. I have approved some of the worst shows in the world, and they ran for almost a decade. But in those early days of television one thing was sure: You always knew in the first two or three weeks whether you had a hit or a failure.

Although Pat was a master at conceiving shows and program formats, he showed little interest in the nuts and bolts of programming. Pat's major concern was in the larger field of broadcasting as a whole. And that suited me perfectly, because I very quickly became obsessed with the mechanics of the television schedule and the effect it could have on a program's ratings. It was an obsession that virtually ensured my survival in a fickle industry in which *everyone*, from the president right on down, was disposable. No executive was ever fired because of good ratings and no career was ever saved by a screening of the Sadler's Well Ballet. The more eyeballs that were fixed to that television screen, the more advertisers were willing to pay. It was as simple as that. And from the early 1950s, ratings began to dominate my thinking.

I had to have the numbers before anyone else. I became compulsive about it. Nowadays, the A.C. Nielsen Company can tell you who is watching a show while they are viewing it. It can even measure the audience drop during commercial breaks. But during the 1950s and 1960s the methods were much cruder. A number of companies supplied the ratings in those days, but A.C. Nielsen very quickly established itself as the yardstick against which all the networks were measured. Nielsen calculated the viewing figures based upon a cross section of television homes that at the time seemed scientific, but today seem almost laughable in both its simplicity and its scale. The figures were compiled in two ways. On the one hand, a sample of 2,200 homes were given a diary to keep note of when the television was on, what channel it was switched to and who was watching. Meanwhile, another 1,200 homes were equipped with a box, called an audimeter, which was attached to the television set and which recorded raw data on television activity. The results from these 3,400 homes were then extrapolated to form the conventional wisdom for the viewing habits of an entire nation.

Naturally, Nielsen did the best it could to keep the sample as diverse as possible, distributing the diaries and audimeters across a range of income groups and regularly changing participants. But I was dubious. First of all, the process was far too basic and the sample far too small to represent the preferences of more than 150 million people. But more frustrating for me was the fact that it took Nielsen so damn long to get me my figures. The audimeter numbers came in once a week. The diaries came in even later. I did not want to know that a spectacular had bombed two weeks after the fact. I wanted to know that night. Better still, I wanted to know while the show was on the air. Thankfully, we had a fine research department at NBC, and my first stop in the morning would be with them to see what clues they could give me about our evening's performance.

Of course, the Nielsens were not just important for monitoring our shows. They told me how many people were watching the competition too, and what percentage of the viewing public we had captured on any given night. As the decade progressed and the viewing audience increased, the science of programming became more and more about the sequence of programs we put on our channel as well as counter-programming whatever was being offered on the other networks. And this was where Pat's introduction of the magazine format and his taking control away from the advertisers freed me to experiment with the prime-time schedule.

In the very early days of television, a large portion of prime time was simply out of our hands; it was the sponsors who decided when and where their programs would run. But as production moved in-house and shows were divided among multiple sponsors, we at the networks became masters of our own schedule. By the end of 1953, Pat was president of the network, with a workload dominated by sweeping broadcasting ideas. I, meanwhile, was becoming more bogged down in the minutiae of programming and began to exert more control over prime time. Each winter, as the deadline for setting the schedule approached, I would draw up a makeshift program board on a large piece of paper, writing the names of our shows in pencil and then the names of the shows I believed our rivals would schedule in boxes down the side. Then, I would begin arranging and re-arranging the shows until I had a lineup that promised the greatest chance of winning the ratings. But here, too, my earliest influences were inspired by Pat.

When Pat arrived at NBC, the schedule was thrown together with little thought to program order or the viewing audience. NBC was good at live drama, so live drama dominated the schedule, even during the early evening when kids were not yet in bed. But kids did not want to watch drama. They wanted fun shows. They wanted comedy. Milton Berle had already proved the drawing power of comedy on Tuesdays. So Pat implemented a strategy to introduce comedy into the schedule every night of the week at 8 p.m., when the kids would be up, giving rise to midweek shows such as *Paul Winchell and Jerry Mahoney*, and *Four Star Revue*, as well as weekend shows such as *Saturday Night Revue* and *The Colgate Comedy Hour*. Likewise, he introduced drama at 9 p.m., to entertain parents once their children had gone to bed.

By the time I started to play a more prominent role in program planning, during the early to mid-50s, scheduling considerations were becoming more complex. CBS started to pull ahead of NBC in the Nielsens in 1952, and by 1955 it had established a clear lead, thanks to shows like *I Love Lucy* and appearances by many of the stars poached during the Paley Raids. Complicating matters even more was the emergence of a third network, the American Broadcasting Corporation, which turned the two-horse race that had defined the early years of television into a fierce, three-way competition.

ABC was led by Leonard Goldenson, the former head of Paramount Theaters, who had bought the tiny network in 1953. ABC had just five owned-and-operated stations and eight affiliates. Since the key to success was ratings, and since ratings could only be as high as the number of affiliated stations carrying network programming, it was at a severe handicap from the start. On its best day, ABC could reach just 35 percent of television homes. Meanwhile, NBC and CBS had a near monopoly on the more than 300 affiliates across the United States. But that did not stop ABC from giving us a good run for our money. Indeed, Goldenson's lack of muscle forced him to look for new ideas, and to strike a deal with Walt Disney that provided a sharp lesson for me about the power children have over the television dial.

During television's early years, most shows were produced on the East Coast, and Hollywood treated television with contempt. The few television shows that were made on the West Coast were almost solely produced by small production companies like Lucille Ball and Desi Arnaz's Desilu Productions, which made *I Love Lucy*. The bigger studio men may have considered themselves above television. But Walt Disney, head of the smaller Walt Disney Studios, was eager to find new opportunities and naturally gravitated towards the networks.

Walt was a man of character. He was both a creative genius and a sound businessman. He genuinely loved children too. His animations enjoyed much-deserved success, but his studios lacked the money to match his ambitions, which included a multi-million dollar Disney theme park that he wanted to build in Anaheim, California. Walt needed money. And since a partnership between a West Coast production studio and an East Coast network seemed to make sense, he flew to New York looking for a deal. The first company he approached was NBC.

We had already broadcast a couple of one-hour Disney specials in 1950 and 1951 to some success, and Walt quite rightly thought the General might be receptive to a deal. His offer was a series of one-hour Disney shows, 20 in all, in return for funding towards the theme park. Walt's only condition was that he got to introduce the shows himself so that he could tell people about his work at the studios, Disney's upcoming features, and his plans for the new California attraction. Perhaps unsurprisingly, the General, who a few years previously had refused to bow to the demands of his stars during the Paley Raids, would hear none of it. Never mind the risks involved in funding the theme park, he was not going to give this studio guy air time on his network. Supported by the sales department, who said *Disneyland* was not a promising show, the General turned it down. Paley and CBS did the same. Which left ABC.

Lagging in the ratings, ABC had nothing to lose. In fact, *Disneyland* perfectly matched Goldenson's hunger for something to differentiate ABC from the other networks. But he did not just take *Disneyland* and dump it anywhere in the schedule. When the show debuted in October 1954, his program department scheduled it for Wednesday night at 7:30 p.m.

It was an exceedingly clever play. Seven-thirty was something of a no-man's land in those days on the major networks. Both NBC and CBS divided the half hour before 8 p.m. between 15 minutes of singing by a well-known performer, like Dinah Shore or Perry Como, and 15 minutes of news. By moving what was essentially a prime-time show back by a half hour, ABC not only captured the kids, it also locked the dial into the network early in the evening, cutting into rival 8 p.m. shows like NBC's *I Married Joan* and CBS's Arthur Godfrey.

Disneyland was a hit with the kids and a smash for ABC. It had the perfect mix of animation, adventure stories and the tales of Davy Crockett, as well as behind-the-scenes footage and teasers for upcoming Disney productions. The following year, as *I Married Joan* disappeared off the air, ABC aired a live spectacular celebrating the opening of the new Disneyland theme park.

The incredible success ABC had in running a kids' show at 7:30 p.m. stuck with me. Years later at CBS I would schedule *The Munsters* at 7:30 p.m. for the same reason: to hook the kids early and hope that the adults followed. I even attempted to take children's or at least family-friendly entertainment all the way through to 9 p.m., with the idea that if you could get the kids to stay with you until 9, there was a good chance their parents would stay even later.

Through ABC's success, and our own hits and misses at NBC, I was gradually learning one of the most basic and yet fundamental lessons in programming: that with very few exceptions, the time and day you schedule a show can be almost as important as the content. *I Love Lucy* was one of the few shows you could put any time and it would be a hit. Lucy was a visual comic who appealed to kids and adults. Her 9 p.m. Monday slot on CBS was neither a help nor a hindrance. She was probably the foremost visual comedienne of our day and one of the greatest television performers of all time. But for most other shows, the schedule could contribute to its success or its failure.

It may seem overly simplistic now, but these were the early days of television. We were barely past the stage of being elated if the sound and picture came out clearly. So the idea of actually thinking about *who* was watching, and *when*, was a sign of real progress. Across the industry, people began to seriously consider the demographics of a time period and the competition on the other side.

Even if a rival network led with a seemingly unbeatable show, it usually presented a counter-programming opportunity. Though *I Love Lucy* was the biggest show in television it was still a situation comedy. So we would throw alternatives against it; one year a musical-variety program, *The RCA Victor Show*, the following year a cutting-edge drama series, *Medic*. Of course, they weren't strong enough to knock *Lucy* off the number-one spot. But they were sufficient to attract a sizable audience that was not in the mood to watch Lucy eating marshmallows or stomping on grapes. We may have got a lower number, but it was enough to satisfy an advertiser. And as my obsession with scheduling grew, it even led to one of my few disagreements with Pat.

Although the spectaculars enjoyed some success, I always felt that they would have scored much higher ratings if they were broadcast on a different day and time. Not only did *Producers' Showcase* go up against *Lucy* on Monday nights, it was scheduled at 8 p.m., which was far too early in the evening. A sizable portion of the audience at that time were kids, who were never going to care for drama, and because of the time difference, our West Coast audience was still on its way home from work. As filmed programming began to take hold later in the decade, time zones became less of a problem. But in the early 1950s it was a real, and very tricky, factor to take into account.

Not that I am trying to make myself out to be a television genius. I could no more have told Pat that *Disneyland* would be a success than I could have predicted Max Liebman's *Satins and Spurs* would be a failure. Television is an inexact science. If you get it right 50 percent of the time, you are a genius. And I made more than my share of mistakes, not least of which was when I was approached by a producer who had an idea to turn the *Lassie* stories into a TV series in 1953.

At the time, we were in the middle of developing color shows for the General, and I was scrambling each month to find material for Pat's spectaculars. *Lassie* sounded like a one-hit wonder at best. I mean, how many times could a goddamned dog save a child from a burning building? I turned the show down and it was snapped up by CBS, where it went on to be a hit for almost 20 years and probably one of the greatest children's shows of all time.

But despite the occasional *Lassie* incident, I was doing well. The General, though he hardly ever spoke to me, seemed to like me and I began to climb the corporate ladder quickly. When I started out in the press department I made $21,000 a year. When they promoted me to a vice president a few years later I was making $34,000 a year. I still have a note at home, scrawled in pen, from the General that just says: "Give Mike Dann More Money." And they did. By the mid-50s I was making $40,000 a year and was responsible not only for overseeing shows and making deals with agents and producers, but also for negotiating contracts with our sponsors. One minute I was signing a new show, the next minute I was on a plane headed for Detroit or Dallas or Dayton, Ohio, trying to convince a toothpaste company that they really needed to put their name to our latest sitcom or docudrama.

The advertising power of television was impossible to ignore. In its early days radio had proven that program sponsorship could turn an unknown product into a goldmine. Television was even more powerful. *Kraft Television Theater* transformed lackluster sales of McLaren's Imperial Cheese into a national favorite. By 1956, advertisers were spending about one billion dollars a year to reach the 85 percent of American homes that owned a television set. And my job was to persuade them that their product was a perfect fit for our latest show.

Entertainment may have been one of the few industries where Jewish people could succeed in the 20th century—the owners of all three networks, Sarnoff, Paley and Goldenson, were Jews. Nevertheless, though the moguls, entertainers and their agents were often Jewish, network salesman and the executives they had to meet with at the nation's largest companies were predominantly WASPs. Deals were brokered over a drink at the country club or during a round of golf. The fast-talking, wisecracking, back-slapping "East Coast" way of doing business was frowned upon.

I have always been good at sales. By the age of 8 or 9 I was making good money selling magazine subscriptions door-to-door for the Curtis Publishing Company. Talking to people, making them like me, and persuading them to buy something they never knew they needed has always come easily. It requires confidence, the ability to think on your feet and a bit of chutzpah. Never more so than in 1954, when I flew out to Midland, Michigan, to see one of our largest sponsors, the Dow Chemical Company.

Dow had just brought out a new plastic product for storing food called Saran Wrap. I had two shows in my pocket, *Caesar's Hour*, which was a surefire hit after the success of *Your Show of Shows*, and a new docudrama series called *Medic*, which was due to premiere in the fall opposite *I Love Lucy*, the number-one show in television.

Midland is one of those company towns, like Hershey, Pennsylvania, or Corning, New York, that rises and falls on the fortunes of one company. In Midland, Dow Chemical was that company. Founded around the turn of the century, Dow was doing extremely well by the mid-1950s, its stock was riding high, and the affluence and beauty of the city were apparent the minute my taxi pulled into town one Thursday afternoon. Many of the most striking buildings, the churches and the library were designed by Alden Dow, a student of Frank Lloyd Wright and the son of Dow Chemical founder Herbert Henry Dow. With "Mr. Big" arriving from New York, the Dow men decided that after my presentation on Friday morning, they would throw a little party and then take me to a football game on the Saturday.

Arriving at the meeting I saw that I did not have too much to worry about. Dow was the perfect company for advertising—bloated and wealthy—and I had already decided that *Caesar's Hour* would be a perfect fit. We were selling a number of spots for the show, and the magazine format was in full swing by now, but I knew they would not mind sharing space with some of America's other large corporations. *Medic* could wait. We did not have high hopes for the show going up against *Lucy*, and I had permission to give the show away if I needed to.

I launched into my presentation, telling the Dow executives about the great ratings Sid Caesar had scored for *Your Show of Shows* and how excited Caesar would be if the great Dow Chemical was to be one of his sponsors, adding liberal references to what a great product Saran Wrap promised to be. About halfway through the presentation I was called to the telephone. It was New York calling to warn me that *Caesar's Hour* had sold out. I was going to have to sell *Medic* to Dow Chemical and I only had a half day to do it.

I returned to the conference room and finished my spiel about what a wonderful show *Caesar's Hour* would be and how great if Dow would be the sponsors.

"Now, fellas, I'm sure *Caesar's Hour* will be great for you," I said. "But I can't help but think that Dow Chemical is more than just a spot on a show. You could buy a spot on any television station. But perhaps Dow should have its own show?

"I came out here to sell you *Caesar's Hour*. But you have a new product. It's got to stand for something! You guys have worked so hard developing this won-der-ful new Saran Wrap.

"Now, we have a new product of our own. It's a show called *Medic*. I don't know if you sell your products to women?… Oh, that's right, it's a consumer product for women… Well, this show is set in a hospital. It's like *Dragnet*. Only with doctors. It's a little bit strong, mind you. The first show is about the birth of a baby. But we think it's going to be a Very. Big. Hit."

There were a few murmurs and a slight shuffling of feet before one of the Dow executives told me, politely, that although it sounded like a decent show, it probably was not for them.

"Okay, fellas. Maybe you're right," I said. "But there's one thing you're forgetting. You're all men. And your customers for Saran Wrap are women. Why don't you get your wives in here and let them take a look before you turn it down."

We met again at 5 p.m., this time with all the executives' wives in tow. We set *Medic* going in a screening room, and 30 minutes later they started to file out. Now *Medic* was a good show. We used some real life doctors and nurses, we based episodes on real events, and we sometimes included footage of actual procedures. The first episode, which we screened for the wives, involved a story-line about a woman who dies during labor and included footage of a live birth. When the wives came out of the screening room many of them were in tears.

"Bob... Larry... Bill... Tom," I could hear them saying, "you've got to buy the show."

I was so happy that night at the Dow party. I was never a big drinker but these guys could put them away. I woke up in the morning feeling so sick that I thought I was going to die. We had to stop at a doctor's office on the way to the football game so that I could pick up some pills. They never once questioned the fact that *Medic* was up against Lucy. And to be honest, as it turned out, the program did pretty well anyway. NBC gave *Medic* a big push in the fall and the show was a minor success. When I arrived back in New York I was never so glad to come home from a trip in my life. And when I met the General's son, Bobby Sarnoff, at '21' he was delighted.

"How did you ever do it?" he asked.

"I don't know, Bobby," I replied. "I guess it's just a great show."

6.

Trouble at the Top

"General, you're sitting in my chair." – Pat Weaver, 1956.

I liked Bobby Sarnoff. He joined NBC around the same time I did, and he worked his way up through various divisions and departments. He was a few years older than I was, and it was obvious from the start that he was being groomed to take over from his father, the General. Pat liked Bobby too. They had been acquaintances before Pat moved to NBC, and Bobby was one of the reasons that Pat accepted the job.

Pat did not seem to mind that Bobby would almost certainly one day leap-frog to the top of NBC. But there was one thing that Pat could not stand, and that was having either of the Sarnoffs, Bobby or the General, meddling in programming decisions that Pat felt were above their capabilities. Pat was not beyond putting either of the Sarnoffs in their place, and the friction only increased as the years went on. It was only a matter of time before somebody had to go. And it was not going to be a Sarnoff.

Pat was such an important part of the RCA machine that it was very hard for the General to fire him. He was one of the foremost television experts in the world. And by the mid-50s, television was the dominant media form. Yet even in radio, Pat was determined not to allow NBC to fall behind. Sometime in 1953 or 1954, Pat turned to me in the office and announced: "Radio's gone. We can't just entertain any more. We've got to do something else. We have to become a service network."

As with the magazine format in television, Pat's new idea for radio was to tear up the 30- or 60-minute radio show, a comedy or drama, and create a 40-hour weekend program that brought a range of genres into the listener's home.

"It's all going to come from one control room," Pat said. "There's going to be plenty of time for local stations to cut in and out, but we're going to have service programming all day long—entertainment, music, comedy, news and current affairs. The stations can take as much or as little as they want."

It was a terrific idea. We called the show *Monitor*, and we arranged for a special control room to be built on the fifth floor of Rockefeller Center. The show debuted in June 1955, with its trademark Morse-code tones—known as the *Monitor* Beacon—ringing out the letter "M."

To keep a show like that running through Saturday and Sunday required an enormous staff. And at one time or another, Pat persuaded some of the greatest broadcasters, journalists and entertainers of the day to appear on *Monitor*: Dave Garroway, David Brinkley, Bill Cosby, Woody Allen, even the future New York Post gossip columnist Cindy Adams. The show was huge. When asked by a reporter to describe it in two words, Pat shot back: "It's a kaleidoscopic phantasmagoria." And ratings were so successful that it literally kept NBC Radio in the black for years to come. The General was thrilled. But of course, that did not stop him from adding his own suggestions for the show in a note he sent to Pat soon after the first episode:

Dear Pat,

I like very much the Monitor show. I think it's a very good idea. But I don't like the Monitor Beacon. It's a very unattractive noise and I think it's annoying. Please remove it.
General Sarnoff.

Now, the *Monitor* Beacon was very important to Pat. He had wanted to give the show a certain technological and international quality, and the beacon was the symbol of the show—it was like a telegraph signal being broadcast around the world. So Pat took a pen and scribbled a single line beneath the General's note:

"Dear General. You're addressing yourself to a subject you're not familiar with. Pat."

"Pat," I said. "You can't send that to the General."

But Pat would have none of it. He called his secretary, Peggy, into the room and told her to put the note in a confidential envelope and send it up to the General.

It was typical of Pat. He was not being mean. He just did not care about anything except broadcasting. He was a man of character. And he treated everyone the same, even the General, which was not the smartest move if he wanted to hold on to his job.

I remember taking part in a meeting with the General and Pat in the mid-50s about the falling cost of color production. The tension between the two was almost unbearable. Pat was being very direct. And the General, obviously frustrated and annoyed that an underling was showing such disrespect, seemed to have lost all patience with his president. Once, when Bobby Sarnoff got overexcited during a meeting, Pat turned to him and said, "Down boy! Down!" To an executive vice president! The General's son! A man who was being groomed to take over NBC one day. (And, I might add, a bit of a putz who would later take RCA down the tubes.)

I never had the courage to stand up to the General—or later to Bill Paley—like that. But at NBC I could definitely be cocky when dealing with agents, producers and, sometimes, colleagues. I was an aggressive young man, and Pat would soon put me in my place. If I misbehaved or stepped out of line he would chastise me, saying things like, "I think you're being rude" or "You're being harsh" or "Give him a break!"

Pat also entrusted me with my first full-time production role, overseeing *Conversations with Elder Wise Men*, which ran from 1952 to 1956. The idea of the show was to compile an archive of interviews with the world's greatest artists and thinkers. One of our earliest guests was Bertrand Russell, and I remember calling our London bureau chief, Romney Wheeler, to instruct him to conduct an interview with the famous philosopher, making sure that only Lord Russell appeared on the screen. This was a little too much for Romney. But after convincing him that the idea of the series was for only the subject to be seen, he went along and conducted one of the most interesting interviews of the series.

Lord Russell was very controversial in England and the United States at this time because of his pacifist views and his opposition to nuclear weapons. When he appeared on the screen, and Romney asked his first question, we were all waiting for a very important pronouncement on the latest issue of the day.

"Lord Russell," Romney asked, "in your whole life, what do you think is the most important thought you've had? What could you tell us to start this program, that would make people understand your thinking?"

Lord Russell, white haired and looking very thoughtful, said to the camera, "Well, I remember as a little boy sitting on the couch at night to wait for the lamplighter coming along the street to light the lamps in our London neighborhood. No matter what time of day it was, my parents would let me sit on the couch because I so wanted to see the lamplighter. He never waved to me; he had many lamps to light. But I always liked to see my friend, the lamplighter, because the whole street would light up and it was exciting.

"Then, one evening, I sat and waited on the couch. But the lamplighter never came. And suddenly all the lights went up at once. I never forgot my friend, the lamplighter, to this day. You know, we still need lamplighters, whether in public office or not, to lead the way. When everything goes on at once, it's different."

As well as producing shows, I was also conducting meeting with agents, producers, writers and stars. As the television production industry became centered increasingly on the West Coast, I began having to make regular trips to Hollywood, starting around 1953. I used to take the overnight TWA flight that left New York in the evening and would arrive in Los Angeles early the following morning. In those days TWA had a luxury plane, called the Constellation, which had six or eight berths. It was very important to get one of the berths on the plane, and if they were all taken I would usually manage to have someone bumped. Likewise, I in turn would get bumped if a star or a big producer or director was on the plane.

The berths gave rise to the plane being referred to by its regular transcontinental passengers as the "15,000-feet-high love boat." And there were often occasions when I would see some of the most famous stars of the day disappear behind the curtain with girlfriends and partners—not that I would wish to invade their privacy by naming them now. Let's just say it provided me with a great deal of entertainment to watch Hollywood's finest disappear in the evening and then exit the following morning trying to appear as though it was the most natural thing in the world.

At the airport I would be met by a driver and whisked by limousine to the Beverly Hills Hotel, a pink Spanish colonial mansion high in the Hollywood hills. During the 50s and 60s, the hotel was one of the most important centers of the entertainment world. Surrounded by beautiful gardens and equipped with a huge tennis court and a large swimming pool, it had everything a star could need, from the storied Polo Lounge, where you could find the most influential industry types of the day discussing shows over cocktails, to a selection of shops on the ground floor catering to the most demanding tastes. A star—or mistress—could spend the night at the Beverly Hills Hotel and emerge the next day in a completely new wardrobe. For men, there was a barbershop, where you might find yourself seated next to Frank Sinatra or Fred Astaire. I remember one major film star who used to give money to the barber so that he could arrange for prostitutes to be sent over to the veteran's hospital, his contribution to those who had given so courageously during the war.

Many of the actors and actresses had to be out at dawn to appear on the studio lot, some as early as 5 a.m., so the stores opened accordingly to cater to them. I used to rise a little later, around 8 a.m., and play tennis between 9 a.m.

and 10 a.m. Katharine Hepburn would often take the 8 a.m. to 9 a.m. slot before me, and as we passed each other on the court she would always nod and say, "Hello, Mr. Dann" and then add something about how well she seemed to be playing that day. For a young man still very much starting out in television it was almost too much to see her breeze past me, perhaps to return to her lover Spencer Tracy. Katharine always remained very gracious to me, and I would use her later in a number of television shows.

Katharine's friendly demeanor was in no small part due to the hotel's tennis coach, the Englishman Harvey Snodgrass, who could hit the ball to the center of your racket every time. I would sometimes watch him make Katharine run from one end of the court to the other, but always within a range that would allow her to return the ball. I suffered with polio as a youth and as a consequence one leg is slightly shorter than the other, so Harvey would go a little easier on me. But the result was always the same: Harvey would leave whomever he was playing with feeling like the greatest tennis player in the world.

After my tennis match I would either take a car out to the NBC offices at Hollywood and Vine or spend the day working beside the pool, using one of the cabanas as a makeshift office. I loved the sun, especially if I was coming from New York in the winter, and I would make sure to bronze slowly as I went over scripts and conducted meetings with producers and writers.

During my initial visits to the hotel, I would stay in one of their rooms. But I quickly gravitated towards my own suite—rooms 176 and 177—where I had a very large bedroom, a large living room, a huge bath, a full-service bar and a patio. At one point my next-door neighbor was Howard Hughes, who had four suites at the hotel, though I never once saw him enter or leave the building, just his employees who would be stationed in one room or another, 24 hours a day. They came in pairs and would eat in the room next door to me. They were polite and would say "Hello," but I never figured out what their purpose was.

Back in New York, the relationship between Pat and the General was becoming increasingly tense. Throughout the early 1950s the legend of Sylvester "Pat" Weaver grew. And though the General may have frowned upon financial excess, his pride did not take kindly to being upstaged by one of his juniors. While the General, who had contributed so much to television, remained relatively unrecognized, Pat was seen, and lauded, as one of the most innovative and daring executives of his day. As Pat's successes grew, so did the attention of the press. In the fall of 1954, The New Yorker ran an extensive, 30-odd page profile of Pat by Thomas Whiteside, who spent months following him around meetings at work. It must have galled the General no end to be overshadowed by an employee, particularly an upper–middle-class intellectual like Pat, who refused to treat the General and his son with deference.

Given their chilly relations it was little surprise when, in late 1955, the General promoted Bobby to president and kicked Pat upstairs to chairman of the board. It was an unofficial "goodbye" for Pat, who was stripped of most of his powers and left as basically little more than an advisor. Though Pat liked Bobby a great deal, Bobby was neither an original thinker nor a very good negotiator. He had emerged from the shadow of a very strong father and learned most of what he knew about television under the tutelage of Pat, a stern teacher. Bobby was a passive person. And it was an unhappy time for Pat to watch, frustrated, as the Sarnoffs tightened their grip on NBC. His reserve cracked soon after the promotions, during the first board meeting under the reshuffled management.

We were all seated in the boardroom with the General in the chairman's seat at the head of the table as usual. But now Pat was the chairman. And when he entered the room he strode purposefully towards the General, stopped, and glaring down at him, said, "General, you're sitting in my chair."

It was very awkward. The General looked up at his angry new chairman, stood and, muttering something under his breath, moved to another seat.

Pat did not last another year. The impotent chairman's post was just too frustrating for such a dynamic man. He resigned in September 1956, one year before Fred Coe and Max Liebman both left NBC, disillusioned with the Sarnoffs' increasing lack of interest in live drama. I would go on to work for almost a dozen more presidents, but none of them came close to Pat. His revolutionary contributions to the television industry, like the magazine format and specials, may have been inevitable, but he hastened their arrival by years if not decades. There would never be another like him.

Pat's departure, like that of Fred Coe and Max Liebman, marked the end of an era. His philosophy about the educational role that television could play in American public life fizzled out within a year or so. His name became poisoned with the industry. No networks or movie studios would take him. When he tried to set up a Pay TV station in California a few years later, he was muscled out of business by theater owners and the networks. Though he continued in the communications business for the rest of his life, it was never at the helm of a company as influential as NBC.

Meanwhile, the popularity of live anthology dramas and spectaculars was beginning to wane. The networks were looking increasingly towards the mass market and the low brow. Although I had a huge amount of sympathy for

Pat, there was some sense in NBC's new priorities. When Pat arrived at NBC, less than a quarter of American homes had a television set. By the time he left, more than three quarters of homes had a television set. The audience was changing. And the emphasis of the programming department was shifting from convincing people to buy a TV or a color TV to attracting the largest possible audience and increasing advertising revenue. We were no longer catering to the wealthy elite. We were catering to the public at large. And mass audiences wanted light entertainment like comedies, dramas and quiz shows.

Pat's departure threw NBC's program department into a tailspin. As a temporary measure, Bobby took over Pat's role as chairman while simultaneously holding the office of president. It was a delicate time, with staff divided between those who had an allegiance to Pat and those who supported the Sarnoffs. On the day that Bobby took over he called a conference of all the senior executives in the sixth-floor boardroom. Around the imposing board table sat about 30 men, with Bobby standing at the head. He delivered a long and earnest speech, pointing out that the program department had been through a fractious period and imploring us to put the past behind us, to work as a team to make NBC the foremost company in the history of broadcasting.

When he finished his speech around 4 p.m., and after the applause died down, I rose and said: "The meeting of the Mike Dann Club for President, scheduled for this afternoon at four thirty, has been indefinitely postponed." And the whole table, which a few seconds before had been nodding in solemn agreement, roared with laughter.

7.

<u>Changing Channels</u>

My days at NBC were numbered. Sure, my situation had been uncertain while Pat and the General were bickering. But without Pat the balance of power weighed heavily against me. Bobby was heir apparent. There was no chance that I could rise much further than my current post as vice president of television program sales. And besides, I had no desire to go much further. I was a programmer, not an administrator. I did not like going to sales and budget meetings. I did not like dealing with personnel problems. I had no urge to testify before the FCC in Washington. That was boring.

I loved meeting with agents and producers, dealing with talent and stars. I loved flying out to Hollywood, staying at the Beverly Hills Hotel and conducting meetings by the pool. I loved meeting Sol Hurok and plotting how we could bring the greatest ballet dancers and musicians to network television. I loved signing shows, scheduling shows and then scanning the numbers as they came in. That was my greatest love, my passion. It was the best job in the business. But it was about to become a whole lot less enjoyable under Bobby Sarnoff.

Though Bobby was a good kid, he was also a man of limited abilities. Soon after Pat left NBC, the talent agency MCA stiffed us by selling one of our top shows, *Wagon Train*, to ABC. The show, starring Ward Bond as Major Seth Adams and Robert Horton as his scout Flint McCullough, was hugely popular and would be a major loss. MCA had a history of putting one over on the Sarnoffs; they had been involved in the Paley Raids 10 years earlier, when we had lost more than a handful of our top stars to CBS. And this was the final straw for Bobby.

"Lou Wasserman and MCA cannot be trusted," he instructed us. "They will never be allowed in our building again."

Shutting out MCA was going to be very difficult for NBC. We relied upon them for so many of our shows. But I could see why Bobby and the General would want to cut their losses and make a point. Then, less than a month later, Bobby called me into his office.

"I've just closed a very big deal, Mike. We're going to have the first ninety-minute Western."

"Oh, Bobby. That's great."

"James Drury is going to star in it and he's going to be the new Western star."

I had no idea who James Drury was. I had never even heard his name before.

"Wonderful, Bobby, who's the production company?"

"MCA."

"Bobby, how'd you ever pull something like this off?"

"Well, I think they felt bad about the *Wagon Train* deal. This new show could've gone any place. But they brought it to us."

Indeed they did. MCA stole our hit hour-long show and replaced it with a second-rate, 90-minute substitute. The show was *The Virginian*. It ran for quite a few years. But it never did as well as *Wagon Train*.

Meanwhile, Bobby brought in a new man to head up NBC's television department, Robert Kintner. Bob Kintner was everything that Bobby was not. He was a tough-as-nails, hard-drinking former newspaperman, who had risen to president of ABC where he had overseen a period of substantial growth. Under Kintner's watch, ABC had broadcast the Army-McCarthy hearings in full, captivating hundreds of thousands of Americans. He had also signed *Disneyland* and the hit Western *Cheyenne*. One look at Kintner's tough face—it was a bit like being in the ring with a boxer—and I knew my life at NBC would never be the same again.

I was a Weaver man and Kintner knew it. I do not think he was particularly hostile to me. But after the stern yet loving care of Pat, Kintner scared me a lot. A few months after he settled into the job I walked into his office to tell him I had just sold four Bob Hope specials to Timex.

"Gee, Mike," Kintner said. "I've just had lunch with Larry Bruff and told him he could have them for Chesterfields."

"Oh dear," I said. "I just sold it this morning… for the price you told me."

There was a pause and Kintner stared hard at his desk. "Are you sure it's closed?"

"We didn't sign any papers. But I gave my word."

Kintner looked disgusted.

"You're making this very difficult for me, Mike."

"I'm sorry. I'll tell Timex there was a mix-up and you had already closed with Chesterfield. You just tell me what to do and I'll do it."

"No, Mike," Kintner said, as though it was the toughest decision of the week. "You go ahead. You make the deal with Timex."

I might as well have handed in my resignation there and then.

In 1958, there were a number of options if I decided to jump from NBC. I could slide over to another side of the business, like the talent agencies, or secure a job at one of the advertising firms. Then there were the rival networks. ABC held little appeal because there was no chance of winning the ratings with such a small budget and limited affiliate network. But CBS, the undisputed number-one network in America… now there was an operation for a winner.

For my wife, Joanne, nothing could have been more terrible than the thought of jumping from one network to another. Joanne and I first met at NBC, where she worked for the husband-and-wife radio team Tex and Jinx Falkenberg. Joanne was a brilliant woman, an upper–middle-class Jewish girl and scholar of Wordsworth and Coleridge, who had attended all the best schools. We fell in love, got married and in a short time moved into a modern home in Thornwood, and later a Tudor house in Chappaqua, where we raised three children: Jonathan, Patricia and Priscilla. Joanne was much more of an intellectual than I was, and she devoted a great deal of her time to reading. We would sit and discuss Emerson and Thoreau on weekend mornings, and she would read passages of the great writers to our children. But as time went on she developed an intense dislike for television. She did not like the television set to be on in the home. And she very rarely allowed me to bring writers, directors or producers to the house.

I knew that when the time came for me to leave NBC, she would have loved me to have done anything but television. Yet I could not think of anything worse. I loved the business. And with word out in the community that I was unhappy, offers started to roll in from various organizations. Then, one day, I heard that Hubbell Robinson, executive vice president of CBS, was interested in speaking with me.

Although Hubbell was not one of the most powerful men at CBS, he had been instrumental in its programming successes in recent years. Hubbell was dedicated to incorporating class into mass entertainment broadcasting. And he was one of the chief reasons why CBS was known as the "Tiffany Network."

Hubbell had been at CBS for about 10 years, having joined the network from Young & Rubicam. He told me that he would like to bring me into the television department but that Paley was against poaching from NBC—a bit rich, I thought, considering 10 years earlier Paley had boosted his ratings by stealing a raft of stars from the General. Personally, I think the real reason Paley did not want to go out on a limb for me was because he did not know who I was. Either way, the door to CBS closed almost as quickly as it opened.

The next best offer on the table came from my old friend Henry Jaffe. Henry had run a talent agency with his brother Saul for many years. But in 1957, he decided to go solo as a producer, and now he was looking for a partner.

Henry already had a couple of lucrative contracts in the pipeline and he needed help running his new agency. A friend and colleague of mine at NBC, the record executive Manie Sacks, told me I would be crazy to turn Henry down. So, against my wife's better judgment, I moved from the network side of the business into production. I had to get out of NBC. And I had a family to support. In 1958, I handed in my resignation and went to work for Henry.

I cannot say whether I was happy to leave NBC. I definitely missed the vitality of the RCA building and the excitement in there. But I was so busy working for Henry that I barely had time to think about it. Almost as soon as I joined the company, I was thrown into the thick of it as Henry brought me in for talks with AT&T about putting on a television variety show along the lines of a popular radio program, *The Bell Telephone Hour*.

It was the type of assignment I lived for, the kind of show Pat would have loved. I immediately called the director Charles Dubin and a musicologist I knew, and said: "I have to make a presentation to the president of AT&T. They want something along the lines of *The Telephone Hour* but for television, so we're going to have to give them something spectacular. I want to incorporate the best that television can offer: dancing groups, operatic sections, Broadway routines. And let's get a big conductor, like Donald Voorhees, to pull the whole thing together."

Voorhees had been the conductor for the radio version of *The Telephone Hour* since the 40s. He thought he was a god, though in actual fact he was a bit of a schmuck. But he was a successful schmuck, and we needed a big personality like that to give the television show some zing.

Charles and I put together a 15-minute audiovisual presentation: Harry Belafonte performing a jazz number and George Balanchine's dancers performing ballet, with Donald Voorhees conducting from the pit. It was the most beautiful presentation in the world, and as I sat next to the president of AT&T and Henry for the screening, I felt sure they would love it.

When the presentation was over the president of the company turned to me and said: "Where would you put this, Mr. Dann?"

"Well, this belongs at nine o'clock on any network," I answered confidently.

"It's a fantastic show, really something else. How many hours could we do?"

"Thirteen, maybe even twenty-six."

"Then let's do it," he said, putting his arm around me. "You want to go to lunch?"

I looked at Henry, who appeared dumbstruck.

"Lunch would be perfect."

When I returned from the restaurant Henry was going crazy that I had been invited to lunch instead of him. But he soon calmed down when I told him we had been offered $125,000 an hour to do the show.

As the contracts were being drawn up for the *Bell Telephone Hour*, we were also working on another project, Shirley Temple's return to television with a one-hour children's television series, in which Temple would narrate or introduce screen adaptations of fairy tales. I threw myself into this project too.

But just as things were starting to take off I got another call from Hubbell Robinson. Apparently, Paley had changed his mind and, now that I was no longer an NBC employee, he wanted me to join the network. I was being offered the position of vice president in charge of all CBS' East Coast programming. It was a dream come true. I had been with Henry only a few months, and I felt like a total jerk leaving him in the lurch.

"You can have the entire *Bell Telephone Hour*," I said. "I don't want any part of it. I love programming. I've got to go."

Some schmuck I was. *The Bell Telephone Hour* ran for another 10 years. Henry made millions off of it. Not only that, he went on to be an even bigger success, with shows like *Goodyear Playhouse* and *The Dinah Shore Show*. But I did not care. I was heading for CBS, the "Tiffany Network," the runaway prime-time leader, a place where I could really shine. And all of the energy I had kept pent up for the past decade under the stern tutelage of Pat Weaver was about to be unleashed.

8.

The Tiffany Network

When I joined CBS in 1958, television was in an altogether different place than it had been just 10 years earlier when I started work at NBC. The mass audience was growing rapidly, and new genres of programming, particularly westerns and quiz shows, were taking over the schedule. CBS led the industry with old favorites like *I Love Lucy* and *Ed Sullivan* as well as newer hits from the latest genres such as *The $64,000 Question* and *Gunsmoke*.

It was a sad time for longstanding CBS employees like the legendary Edward R. Murrow, who had pioneered the serious side of the television industry, first as a CBS radio man during the Second World War filing stirring reports from blitz-ravaged London, and later as the probing host of the controversial *See It Now* documentary news show. During the 1950s, Murrow and his colleague Fred Friendly challenged the nation with programs that exposed the hardships suffered by U.S. servicemen in the Korean War and that highlighted the excesses of anti-Communist hysteria. His power and influence reached new heights in 1954, when Murrow illustrated the absurdity of Senator Joseph McCarthy's Communist witch hunt by broadcasting a show devoted to the Senator's rabid speeches.

But times were changing. Murrow's shows were good for the network image, but they were terrible for ratings and vastly unpopular with sponsors. Quiz shows, on the other hand, were a hit. Within weeks of going on air, *The $64,000 Question* replaced *Lucy* as the number-one show in television. Its sponsor, Revlon, was delighted as sales tripled in the first year alone. By the time I arrived at CBS, Murrow had been relegated to broadcasting a few hour-long *See It Now* specials each year, and relations with the boss, Bill Paley, were strained. In 1958, the very year I joined the network, Murrow gave a speech to the annual convention of the Radio and Television News Directors Association, in Chicago, criticizing the industry for valuing ratings and entertainment over newsgathering and public service:

"This instrument can teach, it can illuminate; yes, and it can even inspire. But it can do so only to the extent that humans are determined to use it to those ends. Otherwise it is merely wires and lights in a box."

It was a warning that I had little time to listen to. I had a powerful position at the top network in the nation, and I intended to use it. I had survived at NBC by following orders and remaining in the background, never pursuing publicity or recognition for any of our successes. I never pushed for my name to be associated with the spectaculars or any other shows. I just got the job done and pushed ahead. But at CBS all of that changed. Without a role model, and in the absence of an authority figure like Pat, I burst into the open. I knew programming. I spoke up in meetings. I talked to the press. I was impudent, insolent, rude. I was not fighting for a higher salary or a better title. I was not even fighting for a better form of programming. I was fighting to keep CBS at the top of the ratings and to keep my job in the company.

I was in charge of CBS's East Coast programming with final say over dozens of shows. The center of entertainment may have been gradually moving west to Hollywood, but in New York we still had major programs like *The Jackie Gleason Show* and *The Ed Sullivan Show*. And the city was still bursting with agents and talent. I ate lunch at the finest restaurants every day—La Caravelle, Le Pavillon, La Côte Basque—often meeting agents from the William Morris office, or my friend Ted Ashley, who had his own Ashley-Famous Agency, or the impresario Sol Hurok to discuss ideas, contracts, shows, talent and, of course, to exchange gossip.

I had the authority to make deals worth hundreds of thousands of dollars with just my word as guarantee. It is incredible to think of the enormous sums that were committed on a handshake alone. But you could never go back on your word, or no one would ever trust you again. During my entire career a deal never stopped after leaving my office. And if I signed the right show and scheduled it at the right time, then it could be worth many times the sum that CBS paid for it. Of course, there were more failures than successes. But that was the business. And I had the confidence from my days at NBC to think quickly and to trust my instincts.

CBS, headquartered at 485 Madison Avenue, was a much more disciplined, if slightly less glamorous, place than the RCA building. The chairman of the company, Bill Paley, was an overbearing personality who during my time at the network alternated between taking minute interest in programming one year and having little, if anything, to do with the company the next. He had grown the firm from a tiny radio interest in the 1920s into the largest and most powerful network in America. He was a titan of the industry, much better known than the General, and he moved in some of the most elegant and respectable social circles.

Yet day-to-day control of CBS lay with a dour character, Dr. Frank Stanton, an upstanding and conservative bureaucrat who cared little for programming but who was very particular about the minutiae of running a giant company.

Stanton had a passion for broadcasting and electronics. While he was a doctoral student at Iowa State University in the early 1930s, he had developed a device for measuring radio usage in the home, a crude forerunner of the boxes used by Nielsen to gather ratings. It was enough to catch the eye of CBS, which offered to fund Stanton's research and, later, gave him a $55 a week job in CBS's then tiny research department. By the late 1930s Stanton presided over a research staff of almost 100 and, after the war, he became president of the entire company.

Stanton was thin and meticulous, stern and proper, kind but firm, and a man of great intelligence. He had a wife but no children. He came into the office on Sundays. He did not have affairs. He was an organizational man, who seemed more interested in restructuring departments and designing the "CBS Eye" logo than in worrying about content. If one of Stanton's secretaries got up to leave her chair, a little light went on in his office so that he knew she was away from her desk.

Though Stanton and Paley had been working closely together for more than 10 years, Stanton always referred to the boss as "Mr. Paley." They never socialized together and as far as I know Paley never invited Stanton over to his house. Paley's social circle consisted mainly of society people, like his wife's brother-in-law, Jock Whitney, plus a few media and entertainment types like Edward R. Murrow and Rex Harrison, to whom Paley always referred as "Sexy Rexy."

Stanton was chief bureaucrat, a key figure for CBS in negotiations with the FCC, and he quickly became a senior statesman within the industry, appearing before Congressional committees and mediating for CBS and the other networks with Presidents Truman and Johnson. Yet Paley never invited Stanton into his home. Sometimes I got the impression that Stanton was terrified of Paley.

Nevertheless, Stanton was one of the few people who regularly went head to head with the boss. When I joined the company one of their biggest disagreements was already brewing. Stanton had been badgering Paley for years about the need for CBS to build a new headquarters. Our offices were small and drab in comparison to the RCA building, and Stanton argued we needed a space befitting "The Tiffany Network." He had even persuaded Paley to buy a plot of land a couple of blocks over on 52nd Street and Sixth Avenue and recommended an acquaintance, the architect Eero Saarinen, to design the building.

But Paley dragged his heels. The vacant land sat empty for years, filled with water, and became known around the office as "Paley's Pond."

In those early days I did not concern myself with the bickering between the two men at the top. I had much more pressing concerns. My immediate bosses were network president Louis Cowan, creator of *The $64,000 Question*, and executive vice president Hubbell Robinson, who was in charge of programming. I got along with Lou very well. But Hubbell and I clashed from the start.

Hubbell was a creative man and a disciplinarian, with a dark, scrunched face that made him look a bit like a Siamese cat. He was a strong advocate for serious television drama, and he was responsible for launching one of the greatest live drama series of all time, *Playhouse 90*. Hubbell expected me to know my place and to wait my turn. But I had other ideas.

During the first major meeting I attended, Paley asked a general question about whether we should spend more time developing shows with strong male leads. Paley was a fan of such characters, especially those of a certain age like James Arness in *Gunsmoke* and Raymond Burr in *Perry Mason*, largely because he liked watching heroes he could identify with, and he wanted to see more of the same on television.

Before anyone could say a word I piped up. I told Paley that although such shows were indeed exceedingly popular, perhaps we ought to look to younger role models too. After all, young people were playing an increasingly important role in society, and some of them no doubt wanted to see younger heroes on their television screens, particularly in the early, prime-time hours.

Paley was intrigued. He started to cross examine me and I answered candidly, back and forth, the way he liked. When the meeting was over I was quite content that I had not said anything to embarrass myself or the department. But that night I got a telephone call from Hubbell asking to see me in his office the next morning.

When I arrived, Hubbell was seated in his chair looking stern as ever.

"Let me get one thing straight," Hubbell said. "When we sit in Mr. Paley's office or boardroom and talk, only one person speaks for the program department. And that's me. Not you."

I nodded and left.

I was supposed to be a puppet and sit quietly. But for once I was not going to do as I was told. Maybe it was because I did not have the same respect for Hubbell as I had for Pat Weaver. Or perhaps it was because after a decade laboring in the industry I wanted my time in the limelight. I like to think that it was because I wanted CBS to win, and I believed I could only do that by offering my opinion. But I admit that I had behavioral issues. I was unhappy at home. I wanted attention. And I was becoming increasingly frustrated in my job under Hubbell.

Whatever my motivation, I had a big mouth and I spoke up whenever and wherever I was. I was rude. And if I offended certain people, I did not care. If Paley asked a question and I thought that Hubbell had gotten it wrong, I told Paley so in front of him. If I wanted to schedule something or bring in a new show, I would argue the point and tell Paley why I liked it. I lost more battles than I won. But slowly I started to get calls from Paley or he would take the time to greet me in the hallway. Though I was a wisecracking junior and Paley could be quite reserved, I think he liked having an executive like me around.

Hubbell very quickly regretted hiring me. He was upset that I dared voice my own opinion. He was tough on me. And we had a rough time arguing about program ideas. Hubbell might have been a creative person but he did not know anything about scheduling. I wanted to build an audience with different kinds of shows—if it worked, it worked!—while Hubbell loved the story form and was more interested in drama.

I was a thorn in Hubbell's side, and he in mine. It got so that I was just waiting to be fired the first chance Hubbell got. He had his own man on the West Coast, Bill Dozier, a real kiss-ass. And I would often find myself outflanked by the two of them. Hubbell routinely vetoed my ideas for shows, like *The Untouchables*, which we lost to ABC. And he was always backed up in his decisions by Bill. Since Bill ran the West Coast, Hubbell saw no reason for me to continue my trips to Hollywood, and my visits to L.A., and to the Beverly Hills Hotel, stopped.

Yet despite all the friction I never for a second doubted that I made the right move in leaving Henry and going to work at CBS. I loved network programming. It was my passion. And as vice president of the East Coast I still had a lot of power, even if I was a good way down the CBS totem pole. I was earning a very decent salary, about $90,000 a year. And I had all the perks: a 14th-floor corner office with a large desk, three television screens, an unlimited expense account, a car at my disposal, and a travel budget that could—and would—take me around the world.

I threw myself into programming. One of my first projects was the music show *Your Hit Parade*, which had been running on NBC for almost 10 years and which had been transferred to CBS for the 1958 season. My first task was to build a capable team. I hired Perry Lafferty, a very able producer who had previously worked mainly on live drama shows. And I singled out a young Canadian, Norman Jewison, to be the director.

My first meeting with Norman did not go so well. He appeared in my office looking slightly disheveled and wearing a pair of sneakers—not the kind of outfit that screamed "give me a job."

I told Norman I wanted him for *Your Hit Parade*. And he told me he did not want to work in New York.

"I'll give you $175 and a new pair of shoes."

"No," said Norman. "The television industry is taking off in Toronto and I'm doing very well there, thank you."

"All right. In addition to that I'm going to find you a nice apartment"—apartments in those days were about $100 or $150 a month—"and you don't have to worry about any expenses."

Norman's sneakers started to shift around a bit.

"Normy," I said. "Stick with me and I'll build you a great staff."

I like to think the shoes and the apartment clinched the deal. Norman stuck around and, along with Perry, went on to do great things—Perry as my right hand at CBS in later years and Norman as a very successful producer-director.

Unfortunately, *Your Hit Parade*, scheduled for Friday nights at 7:30 p.m., did not do so well. The show was supposed to highlight songs that were at the top of the Billboards that week. But music was changing. It was not the Hit Parade of old with simple songs that could be sung by any half-accomplished singer.

Instead, rock 'n' roll was coming into its own. The songs could not be covered by other artists and so they had to be performed by the original singers, who were often more talented at jumping around, jiggling and making a noise than they were at actually singing—at least that is how it seemed to my untrained ears.

Some of the performers were less than attractive too. Their records might have flown off the shelves in the music stores. But they did not appeal to the mass television audience. I could not stand the noise. I said to Perry, "What the hell are you putting on here?" And he said, "Mike, it's not my fault. This is what the kids are buying." It was such a disaster. We took it off the air at the end of the season.

Your Hit Parade was not the only thing to disappear from CBS in 1959. Hubbell Robinson and Lou Cowan disappeared too. Hubbell left the network in disgust at what he saw as the declining standards of programming, particularly the shift away from live drama. He set up his own agency, Hubbell

Robinson Productions, where he hoped to have more freedom to create higher quality shows—though whether *Thriller* and *87th Precinct*, which both ran briefly on NBC, merited the label "quality" is for others to decide. He was replaced at CBS by Oscar Katz, a very strict program researcher and a great contributor to television.

Lou was forced out under more unhappy circumstances. His tenure as president had been in some doubt ever since 1957, when the quiz scandal erupted amid allegations that contestants were being coached and questions manipulated. Lou had risen to president at CBS largely because of his successes with *The $64,000 Question* and its spin-off *The $64,000 Challenge*. With the integrity of the shows in doubt, so too was the integrity of the president.

Quiz shows were the original reality TV. They presented the American public with a succession of average people facing agonizing choices every week. Contestants appeared in cramped studios and soundproof booths, in front of hushed, anxiety-ridden audiences, pausing and thinking, sweating and shaking, as they battled their way up the money tree ever closer to the holy grail of the big money prize. But they would not have made compelling television if not for one important fact: the audience had to relate to the contestants. And the only way to ensure that was to cheat.

Quiz show producers found a number of ways to rig the competitions and boost ratings. They coached contestants, fed them targeted questions and persuaded people to win or lose. They manufactured nerve-wracking ties and exhilarating running streaks to keep the audience coming back for more. In 1956, 50 million people tuned in to NBC's *Twenty One* to watch Charles Van Doren knock out Herbert Stempel in a nail-biting finale that had been decided days before the program went on air.

NBC's quiz shows *Dotto* and *Twenty One* were the first to collapse as, slowly, contestants came forward alleging foul play. A grand jury was convened to look into the allegations but its findings were never made public. Finally, under pressure from millions of people who were dying to know how and by whom they had been cheated, Congress decided to investigate.

During very public hearings, held by the House Subcommittee on Legislative Oversight, accusations were made that *The $64,000 Question* and The *$64,000 Challenge* were both rigged by the sponsor, Revlon. No one ever proved that Lou had anything to do with the apparent conspiracy, but the association was enough.

Lou was ill in hospital at the time. He was a good friend of mine, a fine and dignified man. I had no doubt that he would never have been party to the rigging. And anyone who said he must have known could not appreciate just how many hours Lou was working in those days.

Regardless, Stanton said Lou had to go. He told him to resign and since Lou was actually quite ill at the time, he instructed him to cite ill health in his decision to step down. Lou resigned. But he made sure the papers knew that he was not jumping, he was being pushed. His replacement, Jim Aubrey, terrorized me for the next six years.

9.

Working for the Cobra

"The mere mention of Aubrey's name was enough to make a strong man's blood congeal. Whenever the superboss visited the West Coast, a deadly atmosphere, a coiling miasma, settled over Television City. On these occasions, staff would huddle in their offices and pray they would be spared a face-to-face meeting with the austere and frequently caustic CEO." – Perry Lafferty's unpublished memoir, "Et Tu, Boob Tube."

During my 60 years in the television industry, I have worked with drunks and drug addicts, prima donnas and bullies, thieves, liars and cheats. But not a single one of them has ever come close to hurting me as much as my former boss, CBS president James T. Aubrey Jr. I worked for Aubrey—a tyrant, possibly even a psychopath—for six fearful years, scrambling to defend my professional, emotional and physical well being.

To look at Aubrey you would never have guessed the monster that lay within. He was tall, slim, athletic, attractive, maybe even dashing, in a Hollywood way, with piercing blue eyes and a perfect waist. He was 6 foot 2 inches, a fitness fanatic who skied, played tennis and worked out religiously; he was known semi-affectionately around the office as "Jungle Jim." When he entered a room, my first thought was often, "My gosh, he's handsome."

Aubrey joined CBS in 1958 as an executive vice president working alongside Dr. Frank Stanton. He came to us from ABC, where he had just completed a very successful stint as head of programming. Before that he had worked for CBS as manager of its West Coast programming division. When Lou Cowan was fired in 1959, Aubrey seemed the perfect replacement.

He was clean, neat, presentable, always dressed in a dark, custom-made suit. He attended Phillips Exeter Academy and Princeton. His father was a senior executive at J. Walter Thompson and his wife, Phyllis Thaxter, an actress. He was a great talker, a mesmerizing personality and an accomplished broadcaster. But as the staff of CBS soon found out, he was not the charismatic leader he had seemed.

Quickly, he established a reputation for meddling in the smallest detail of a production, picking over scripts each week and demanding myriad changes from costume and props to characterization and dialogue. He tried to have the actress Barbara Luna taken off a project because she looked too Spanish; he ordered an episode of *Route 66* rewritten because he worried it might offend the John Birch Society. The novelist Merle Miller, contracted to write a pilot for an Aubrey-commissioned series starring Jackie Cooper and Barbara Stanwyck, was forced to toil through 19 drafts before the president eventually dropped the show—but not before the budget ballooned to an estimated $400,000.

When I showed Aubrey a pilot for a new courtroom drama called *The Defenders* in 1961, his reaction was typical: He said the subject was dull. And although he liked E.G. Marshall and Robert Reed as the father-and-son lawyers Lawrence and Kenneth Preston, he could not stand Reed's on-screen wife, Jessica Tandy. The series could go ahead, he told me, only if Tandy was written out of the scripts. I did as I was told and had Tandy removed from the project. Although *The Defenders* went on to become wildly successful, and one of the shows of which I am most proud, I have often wondered whether Tandy, an extremely accomplished actress, could have made it an even better show by providing a counterweight to the two men.

But the damage inflicted by Aubrey's meddling was nothing compared to his temper.

To be sure, he could be charming, gracious and warm. But the next minute he could be a killer. His moods swung wildly. His rage was uncontrollable. One minute he was calm, the next he would explode. In meetings he would think nothing of bawling out an executive or a producer, leaning over his desk barking and screaming. Sometimes, it did not even matter if the person had been at fault. If they happened to be in the wrong seat at the wrong time they were on the receiving end of his wrath. I quickly noted that the worst place to sit in any of these meetings was directly in front of the boss, and over time I gravitated towards the side or behind Aubrey to increase my odds of being safe.

Even worse than Aubrey's temper was his reputation for calmly and cold-bloodedly ending projects and careers. One minute he was telling you how wonderful you were, the next minute you and your series were out the door. In one often whispered-about case he allowed an executive to deliver a half-hour presentation before telling him he was fired. He was not known around the office as the "Smiling Cobra" for nothing.

Of course, there were many times Aubrey got mad at me. But in general I managed to avoid confrontation by keeping my head low and visiting the West Coast as often as possible. Nevertheless, the tension played havoc with my nerves, and in the early 60s I increased the frequency of my trips to my psychoanalyst, Dr. Fisher, from three to four times a week, dashing out the door for my 2 o'clock appointment to lie on a couch and unburden myself of the pressures of working for Aubrey.

But aside from the couch and the Coast, there was nowhere to hide. Aubrey's contempt extended to the very top of the company, to Bill Paley himself, whom he treated like a fool.

To this day I do not know why, but Aubrey's reign at CBS coincided with a period in which Bill Paley took less of a driving role in the network. According to his unofficial biographer Sally Bedell Smith, it was because Paley was more concerned with his health—his doctors spotted a shadow on his lungs in 1959 that turned out to be a false alarm—than the network. She also suspects it was because he was in awe of Aubrey's looks, his WASPish ways and his mesmerizing personality.

Whatever the reason, the once-bullish network chief became a lamb. And Aubrey, perfectly positioned with his office in between Stanton's and Paley's on the 19th floor, was there to take up the slack.

It was typical for Aubrey to talk down to the boss behind his back and even to put him in his place now and again during meetings. In those days, Paley chaired a huge programming meeting twice a month at which Aubrey, along with his programming chiefs, would lay out the department's ideas in front of the chairman, Stanton, the news and current affairs guys, the sports department and the engineers. In these meetings, everyone, Frank Stanton included, referred to the chairman as "Mr. Paley," except Aubrey, who insisted on calling him "Bill."

At one particular meeting, Paley raised the issue of color broadcasts and the fact that NBC, which was then way ahead of CBS in color production, was offering producers a $15,000 subsidy per hour for color shows.

"Jim," Paley said. "Do you think we ought to be doing something like that?"

"Bill," said Aubrey, "There are fifty million television homes. Only four million have color sets. Color is not going to work."

In Hubbell's day I might have argued the case, but not with Aubrey. As I left the room I turned to my colleague Jerry Leider, who was then executive in charge of specials at CBS but who went on to become a successful movie producer, and said, "I think that's the first dumb thing I heard Jim Aubrey say."

The Bill Paley of old would never have countenanced such insubordination in front of his troops, even if his president was right. But Paley sucked it up, as he did the increasing number of times when Aubrey displayed outright contempt. In fact, as time went on our twice-monthly meetings only took place once a month as Paley spent more and more time at his holiday home in the Bahamas.

Meanwhile, Aubrey unleashed his contempt on affiliates, agents, writers and producers. He was brusque, high-handed and mean. He walked out of screenings, script discussions and meetings, sometimes without uttering a word or even deigning to tell people he was not coming back.

He put everyone in their place. They had to know *he* was the boss.

While Aubrey could control most people, celebrities made him feel particularly uneasy, probably because their enormous bank accounts and fawning entourage insulated them from the harsher realities of life.

But Aubrey stubbornly refused to buddy up to the stars as most of his contemporaries did. As far as he was concerned he was the main attraction. And the quicker he could put a celebrity down, the better.

He stuck the knife in however he could, usually by aiming for a celebrity's major weakness—their insecurity about their own work. He would critique shows, whether it was the truth or not, just to bring the star down a peg or two. He would never turn to Jack Benny or Lucille Ball, for example, and say, "You know, I like the show, but maybe you could do it a little bit the other way." That was not in his vocabulary. Instead, he would say, "I saw the show last night and, my God, it stinks."

The stars were his meat. And even with all the power that celebrities had, their careers were often so tied to the network that there was little they could do but suck it up too. Lucille Ball, Danny Thomas and Jack Benny hated him and would gladly have seen Aubrey tossed out of 485 Madison Avenue. But with CBS well ahead in the ratings in the early 1960s, there was little hope of Aubrey being shown the door. He was 101 percent *meshugganah*. But he was bringing in record net profits—between 1959 and 1964 they doubled from $25 million to almost $50 million.

Aubrey's success, however, came at a cost—and not one that could be measured in dollars or ratings. It was the prestige of the network. Within just a few years, he transformed CBS from the leading network, renowned for its quality programming, into the market leader in crass entertainment. For if previous executives, like Lou Cowan and Hubbell Robinson, had tried to maintain at least a modicum of quality along with CBS' lead in the ratings, Aubrey made sure we went for the lowest common denominator time and again.

Nowhere was this more apparent than our dominance of lowbrow entertainment. We gorged ourselves on *Gomer Pyle, U.S.M.C.*; *Mister Ed*; *The Real McCoys*, and *Andy Griffith*, not to mention the well-crafted, if rather stilted, output of writer/producer Paul Henning, who provided us with three of our biggest hits of the decade: *The Beverly Hillbillies* in 1962, *Petticoat Junction* in 1963 and *Green Acres* in 1965.

Under Aubrey's watch, CBS, once regarded as "The Tiffany Network," became known disparagingly as "The Hillbilly Network."

As the label suggests, *The Beverly Hillbillies* was at the vanguard of our domination of the ratings. The program, about a hick family from the Ozarks who become millionaires after striking oil, was the number-one show for years. Even after it slipped from first place, it maintained a top-10 position for almost a decade. It is still on the air in syndication today. But my God, was there ever a worse show in the history of television than *The Beverly Hillbillies*?

The cast were all nice enough people: Buddy Ebsen as Jed Clampett, Irene Ryan as Granny, Donna Douglas as Jed's daughter Elly Mae and the strapping Max Baer as his nephew Jethro. But the comedy was so bland, so staid, so unimaginative that I could not bear to watch it. When Herbert Brodkin later told a reporter that television had reduced the audience "to a bunch of monkeys asking for the same peanuts," he could easily have had *The Beverly Hillbillies* in mind. Aside from the pilot, I did not watch a single episode.

But it was a successful formula. So it was repeated time and again, just as the networks had done with westerns and quiz shows.

The allure of such rural-themed shows was obvious: It was recognizable to the majority of our audience. Sure, you could set a variety show or a current affairs program in New York. After all, New York was where the stars were and where the news was made; it was only natural that *Ed Sullivan*, *Today*, or *Tonight* originated there. People expected the bright lights and the big city then. But if you were telling a story about a family, or a little boy or a little girl, the viewer wanted to see suburban or rural life, because that was where they felt safe.

To the majority of Americans, New York was an okay place to visit, with the tall buildings, the Statue of Liberty, Fifth Avenue and Broadway, but you would not want to live there. The people there were rude, always rushing and pushing each other around. It was big and dirty, smelly and dangerous. It was the Big Apple that nobody wanted to bite. And that same attitude carried over into television.

For that reason, middle America was the setting for almost all of our comedy shows, not just the Hillbilly comedies, but also programs like *The Andy Griffith Show*, set in the fictional Mayberry, North Carolina, and *Father Knows Best*, set in the Midwest. In the 1960s even Lucille Ball found herself in a new setting.

While *I Love Lucy* had been set in an Upper East Side brownstone, *The Lucy Show* was set in Danfield, Connecticut.

The Beverly Hillbillies worked because, although it was set in L.A., it still had a rural ethos, centering on a family of simple folk trying to navigate the pitfalls of wealth and life in the big city. It was a hit in the Midwest, the Southwest and the Far West. It did not do so well in New York. But it was top of the ratings and that was all that counted.

I cannot blame Aubrey for this concentration on the numbers. I was just as guilty in my quest for the ratings. But I at least tried to introduce a little bit of prestige into the schedule, by putting together specials using Sol Hurok's stars or by using other contacts to procure the talents of people like Olivier and Hal Holbrook. But Aubrey was not interested in specials at all. They interfered with the schedule. They were unnecessary. And Aubrey brooked no dissent.

Looking back, it was perhaps ironic that he rose to power at exactly the time that television was coming under increasing criticism for a perceived decline in standards.

During the late 1950s, Pat Weaver, Fred Coe and Edward R. Murrow had all voiced their disapproval of what they saw as the deterioration of television. Now, it was the turn of the head of the FCC, Newton Minow, to give the industry a piece of his mind.

I was not present at the meeting of the National Association of Broadcasters in Washington, D.C., on May 9, 1961. But I did not need to be there to hear what Minow had to say. His speech, which described the television schedule as a "vast wasteland," reverberated across the industry. It was seen as a slap in the face to the assembled heads of the major networks, whom Minow now challenged to sit down for a day and watch their network from beginning to end.

Minow was right. Between 1950 and 1960, great experiments had taken place in television. But as audiences rose and advertising dollars flooded the networks, the schedule was becoming ever more bland. A truly great network, like the BBC in the U.K. for example, broadcast for *some* of the people *most* of the time. But, increasingly, the major U.S. networks were broadcasting for *most* of the people *all* of the time. There was nothing else for it when our scheduling considerations were so dominated by the Nielsens.

What worried Newton Minow so much was that we were using this powerful instrument—television—to force feed the lowest common denominator into people's homes night after night. It was a call to arms that we should have responded to. But we were too busy looking at the numbers to take notice.

There were headlines and a heated public debate. But it did nothing to change programming.

The fact of the matter was that Newton Minow had no real power. He was only the head of the FCC. With the exception of the McCarthy period, I never knew of any outside influence that altered the course of programming more often and more effectively than the Nielsens. They were all we cared about. And so long as Aubrey was bringing in the numbers and the advertising revenue, Paley and Stanton did not give a damn what Newton Minow thought or said— or how much we, as Aubrey's underlings, suffered.

Aubrey's approach to programming was simple: Give the audience what they want. Meanwhile, he wanted everything his way. He wanted it done quickly. And he did not want to hear anybody's advice. It was a minor miracle that shows of any substance made it onto the schedule during his reign. But they did.

The Defenders was my first triumph. I had first heard about the program via my good friend Ted Ashley, and it was one of the first pilots I had made after joining CBS. Produced by Herbert Brodkin and written by Reggie Rose, it was an East Coast show straight out of the mold of the live anthology dramas and had first aired as a two-parter for CBS's live anthology show *Studio One* in 1957.

Brodkin assured me that he was going to get only the best writers, who would tackle the most pressing social issues of the day: racism, euthanasia, abortion, the death penalty, freedom of speech, all set in the cut-and-thrust atmosphere of a courtroom. It was one of the most exciting and socially conscious shows that I ever put on television. It caused no end of controversy, but I did not care. I was proud to have been a part of it.

And yet it could all have ended so easily. Even after I conceded to Aubrey's demand to cut Jessica Tandy, he was still unhappy with the show and decided to put on another program, *Mr. Broadway*, instead. When *Mr. Broadway* did poorly in the ratings, even Paley started to question the programming decision. At one of our regular programming meetings he turned to Aubrey and said, "Do you like that *Mr. Broadway*? Because I'm not so fond of it, and the public doesn't like it. What happened to that other show you had? Let's go with *The Defenders*."

Aubrey's face went bright red. But there was nothing he could do. After it went on the air, *The Defenders* performed better than anything I could have expected and ran for four successful years, a considerable amount of time for a series of that caliber.

Brodkin was the Fred Coe of his day. During the 1950s he had produced
a succession of marvelous anthology dramas for *Studio One* and *Playhouse 90*.
He was a man of few words, tempestuous and difficult to handle. And boy, did
we have some arguments. At one point he did not speak to me for a couple of
years. But he was talented. And during the 1960s we sought those talents for a
number of projects, including two series, *The Nurses* and *Coronet Blue*.

Reggie, meanwhile, was among the handful of top writers of his day in
the same vein as Rod Serling and Paddy Chayefsky. During the 1950s he had
been responsible for one of the greatest dramatic shows of all time, *Twelve
Angry Men*, which he wrote for *Studio One* and which went on to become a
marvelous film starring Henry Fonda and Lee J. Cobb. He was a staunch New
York liberal, who took the then-controversial view that women were equal to
men, that black people were equal to white people and that immigration was
a benefit to our country. I remember one particular episode of *The Defenders*
which dealt with an abortion and which caused such a fuss that a number of big
advertisers pulled sponsorship, some affiliates refused to carry the program and
I was inundated with angry telephone calls. As it happens, the protagonist of
that particular episode decides to keep the baby. But the mere fact that abortion
had been defended in a courtroom on a TV show caused a big ruckus.

Despite the complaints, the show was huge. In many ways it was the exception that proves the rule. Though mediocrity usually wins the ratings, *The
Defenders* was one of the few instances when a quality series won both a high
rating and critical acclaim. It was one of the most talked-about programs of the
day, and it won a number of awards. The acting was marvelous, E.G. Marshall
was superb and so was Robert Reed.

But it was a small victory in a never-ending struggle to get my shows on
the air and to avoid Aubrey's anger. As the years went on, the atmosphere at
the office became unbearable. The pressure was immense, and my increasingly
strained relationship with my wife meant that home was providing little respite
from the strains of the day. My trips to Hollywood began to occur much more
regularly, until eventually I found myself visiting the West Coast twice a month,
for five- or six-day stretches, taking refuge in my large suite at the Beverly Hills
Hotel.

Only on the West Coast could I relax, get some sun, and keep my career
on track. Despite the layer of management above me, I was now something
of a big shot. For the next five or six days I would be chauffeured between my
suite at the Beverly Hills Hotel, my office at Television City, and L.A.'s finest
restaurants. Agents and their stars, aspiring actors and actresses, all wanted to

know me. The guys treated me like I was one of them. The girls thought I was charming. My jokes were the funniest they had ever heard. It was a false world of fake smiles and flattery. But compared to New York and Chappaqua it was heaven. And I drank from it to the very last drop.

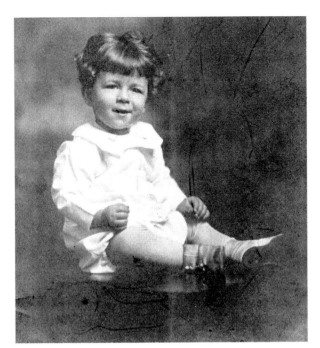

Mike age 2, 1923.

Mike, May 28, 1968. CBS/Landov

Stars of the CBS television series *M*A*S*H* are (L-R) Alan Alda as Capt. Benjamin Franklin 'Hawkeye' Pierce, Wayne Rogers as Capt. John 'Trapper John' McIntyre and Lorett Swit as Maj. Margaret 'Hot Lips' Houlihan. CBS/Landov

Cast members of the CBS television series *Hogan's Heroes*, July 9, 1968. CBS/Landov

Cast members of the CBS television series *The Beverly Hillbillies.* CBS/Landov

Lucille Ball, Don Briggs, and Vivian Vance in the CBS television series *The Lucy Show*, January 10, 1963. CBS/Landov

Mike dining with Sol Hurok at La Caravelle, 1970

Michael Dann (far right) at the Academy of Television Arts and Sciences,
October 14, 1965. CBS/Landov

Pianist Vladimir Horowitz performs on the CBS television program
A Television Carnegie Hall Concert, August 21, 1968. CBS/Landov

At the Peabody Awards 1968 (L-R) Dean John Drewry, Ed Sullivan, Mike Dann, and
Eric Sevareid.

The Judy Garland Show featuring Barbra Streisand &
Judy Garland, October 4, 1963. CBS/Landov

Danny Kaye performs in The *Danny Kaye Show,* August 17,
1963. CBS/Landov

Tom and Dick Smothers perform in *The Smothers Brothers Comedy Hour,* September 20, 1968. CBS/Landov

Mike with Tom and Dick Smothers.

Mike in his office after his promotion to senior vice president of programming, 1965.

James Aubrey, CBS Television City in Los Angeles, September 21, 1961.
CBS/Landov

CBS President Dr. Frank Stanton poses with an architectural model of the CBS headquarters building 'Black Rock', New York, 1961. CBS/Landov

'Black Rock', the CBS Headquarters in New York City. CBS/Landov

10.

The Entertainers

"TV is for idiots! I don't like it... it has lowered the standards of the entertainment industry considerably. You... work years building routines, do them once on TV, and they're finished. Next thing you know, you are too... When and if I ever do my own TV show, I'd like it to be a half-hour on film." – Danny Thomas, 1952.

It must have been sometime in late 1961 or early 1962, I don't remember precisely, when I received word that Lucille Ball wanted to speak to CBS. During the 1950s, while I was at NBC, Lucy had been my nemesis. So it was with great pleasure, and not a little surprise, that I found myself sitting in my office at 485 Madison across from Lucy and her lawyer Mickey Rudin as she told me that she wanted to return to television.

Lucy's first decade at CBS had been an enormous success, not just for the network but also for herself. No one could have predicted what a tremendous hit *I Love Lucy* would be. When Desi and Lucy first came to the network with their idea for the show, CBS had quite rightly hedged its bets. Desi and Lucy were demanding that, unlike most shows which were broadcast live, *I Love Lucy* would be shot on film. The network agreed on condition that Desi and Lucy bore the brunt of production costs and took a pay cut in return for 100 percent ownership of the show. Following *I Love Lucy's* stunning run between 1951 and 1957, and with the show in syndication and reruns, Desi and Lucy were millionaires.

The solitary cloud that hung over their success was that they were no longer happy together. Desi had problems with drink and drugs, and he was a notorious womanizer. By the time Lucy appeared in my office, the couple had divorced and Lucy had bought Desi out of their company, Desilu Productions. So now I was sitting across the table from not only one of the most successful entertainers of the day, but also the first female head of a production studio and one of the smartest businesswomen of the time. With the exception perhaps of Oprah Winfrey and Barbara Walters, no woman has influenced the entertainment industry more than Lucille Ball. In fact, you could say that Lucy paved the way for women like Oprah to rise to the position they enjoy today.

Lucy explained that her idea for the new comedy series would be set in a bank. As she described the story I sat rapt, not so much listening to her ideas as admiring this charming, gracious and smart lady. She had an infectious personality. And I thought to myself, it really does not matter what she wants to do, it is sure to be a hit. Her lawyer, Mickey Rudin, was a large, fearsome man who represented Sinatra and, rumor has it, a number of underworld figures. But he was decent enough and the conversation continued pleasantly. Lucy said she wanted her old slot back, 9 o'clock on Monday nights. But I told her that Danny Thomas was in it and I could think of no reason to move him. The best I could offer was 8:30. She accepted. And, as she left, she looked thrilled.

"Next time you come out to Hollywood," she said. "I am going to cook you a special dinner. It's going to have to be a little late because I don't get home until the early evening and I have to help my children with their homework. But you're going to love it. How do you like roast chicken?"

No sooner was she out of the office than I picked up the phone to Paley.

"Jesus, Mr. Paley. Lucy wants to come back. She's already got a cast together and she wants to work in a bank. Is that okay?"

"Well, how's she going to be without Desi?"

"She's a visual comic. She doesn't need Desi. I think it'll be a wonderful show."

"I agree," said Paley. "There's no question. We want Lucy back."

My next trip out to Hollywood I took a car over to Lucy's house. She had recently remarried a borscht belt comedian called Gary Morton, who was a bit of a putz. But we had a wonderful time. Lucy made roast chicken and mashed potatoes and was fussing around me like a mother hen. I found out that not only had she prepared the meal after a full day's work and going over homework with the kids, but that, as always, she had to be up early the next morning to do her calisthenics before making sure her children were fed and packed off to school.

Lucy was the same at Desilu Studios as she was at home. She was always fussing around the cast, making sure they were ready for their run-throughs and that the producer and director were comfortable. She planned everything, making sure there was always coffee and a Danish available for everyone in the morning. She was the consummate professional. She always knew her lines. And I do not remember once hearing her complain. The only time I ever knew her to be upset was if she thought the show had not gone well, and she would call me after the broadcast and say, "I'm not so sure about that one, Mike. What do you think? Did you like it?"

But Lucy had no need to worry. *The Lucy Show*, which first aired in the fall of 1962, was very successful and ran for six years. I had very little direct involvement in the program once it got off the ground. I left that up to our team on the West Coast. But I kept in constant contact with Lucy and with our West Coast vice president, Hunt Stromberg. Of course, *The Lucy Show* could never match the numbers for *I Love Lucy*. But we never expected it to. CBS had its star back, the ratings were good, and we could not have asked for more.

As a general rule, comics are the most difficult entertainers to deal with. They are often dark, depressive and terribly insecure. But Lucy was nothing of the sort. If anything, she was the opposite.

Jackie Gleason on the other hand was a nightmare, possibly the most difficult person I ever had to deal with. Jackie was more than just a comic. He was an actor, a composer, a writer, perhaps the greatest untrained—and untamed—natural talent in the history of broadcasting. He was so versatile and so talented, equally at home playing dramatic roles in *The Time of Your Life* on *Playhouse 90* or in the movie *The Hustler* as he was playing the comic in *The Honeymooners*. By the time I became deeply involved with Jackie in 1962, he was probably at his peak. He was a formidable talent and one of the nation's best-loved stars.

Jackie was so important to CBS that we built a fancy, circular mansion for him overlooking the woods on the outskirts of Peekskill, New York, that cost about $150,000. He was the only guy who quit three shows at their height and could get away with it. During the 1950s he had enjoyed tremendous success with the *Jackie Gleason Show* and then *The Honeymooners*. In the 1960s he had a short-lived quiz show and a talk show. But in the winter of 1962, he decided to resurrect the old *Jackie Gleason Show* and we scheduled it for 7:30 p.m. on Saturday nights that fall, where it went on to be another great hit.

Ratings aside, Jackie was a problem—or at least his drinking was. One of his drivers told me it was not uncommon for him to booze all night long and then stagger out to the car in the morning to be taken either home or to a nearby hotel. Nothing was more important to Jackie than propping up the bar. And he was damned if he was going to waste valuable time reading scripts and in rehearsals.

This was brought home to me one evening when I was passing by our studios in New York and saw Frank Fontaine, who played "Crazy" Guggenheim in the "Joe The Bartender" sketch, pacing the sidewalk. Each week, Frank would appear following one of Jackie's monologues and deliver some dumb monologue of his own while Jackie did a series of "takes" for the camera, rolling his eyes or looking impatient or annoyed.

I said, "Frank, for heaven's sake, why aren't you rehearsing with Jackie? You should be in dress rehearsals by now."

"This is dress," Frank said.

"Where's Jackie?"

"He never rehearses. He just does takes."

Poor Frank. Apparently, most weeks Jackie simply refused to turn up.

He did not even care about his lines. I remember one Friday, the writers brought me a script ahead of Saturday's rehearsals, asking if I would take it along to Jackie, who was staying in a hotel at 59th and Columbus Circle. Since it was mid-morning, well before Jackie was likely to have started drinking, I hurried over to the hotel and, not wanting to disturb him, tapped on the door and said, "Jackie? Jackie? Look, here's the script from the boys," and shoved it through the mail slot in the door. I hung around in the corridor to see if he might poke his head out of the room. But there was no Jackie. Instead, about five minutes later, the script came flying out the slot in the door.

The guy simply did not give a damn. He was so talented that he often got by just repeating the same material again and again. People loved it. In 1964, when he decided he had had enough of New York and wanted to move the show to Florida, CBS gave in straight away. Jackie loved playing golf, so he decided the best place to live would be near Doral Country Club. The network paid for another new house and to move the entire production of *The Jackie Gleason Show* to Florida.

About every third week I would get a call in the early hours of the morning from Jackie, sounding half awake: "Pal, I'm in big trouble. I've got to see you."

What could I do? I would rush to the airport early in the morning from Chappaqua and catch the next flight down to Florida, where a car would take me straight to the Doral Country Club. I would usually find Jackie sitting in his golf cart. He would have this look of total surprise on his face. In the best case scenario, he would say, "Glad to see you, pal. Get in the cart." Other times, it would just be a straight, "What are you doing here?"

We would go around a couple of holes and then Jackie would ask if I wanted a drink. We would retire to the club around 2 o'clock, where Jackie would order a double something or other and I would have a tuna fish sandwich. Then around 5, I would get back on a plane and fly back to New York.

The Jackie Gleason Show was a strong variety program in a period that was dominated by sitcoms. For if the 1950s had been an era of musical-variety shows, then the 1960s was the decade when sitcoms came into their own. During the 1963-64 season, 13 of the top 15 shows on television were comedies. They were the bedrock of CBS's winning schedule—from the *Beverly Hillbillies* to *The Munsters*. Nevertheless, variety still played an important role, not just in our numbers but also in raising the prestige of the network. And for the upcoming 1963-64 season, CBS signed two of the biggest variety stars of the day, Judy Garland and Danny Kaye.

It was Ted Ashley who brought me the idea for *The Danny Kaye Show*. Danny had already starred in a number of moderately successful specials on CBS. And while I was confident that he could do well in the ratings, I had some reservations about his personality, particularly his reputation for being a pain in the ass. Guiding such a talent each week would require a producer who was both patient enough and stubborn enough to see the project through.

My first choice was Bob Banner, who had worked on *The Dave Garroway Show* and *The Dinah Shore Show*. But Kaye's reputation preceded him, and Banner declined. My second choice, Perry Lafferty, had already acquitted himself very well on a number of shows, including *Your Hit Parade* and variety shows such as *The Andy Williams Show* and Rock Hudson's *The Big Party*. He had proven himself a more than competent producer, and I felt that in the case of Danny Kaye in particular we would benefit from his delicate, yet firm, hand. My instincts proved correct: Danny turned out to be a demanding employee and Perry a master manipulator.

The show itself was both a tremendous challenge and a tremendous success. Not only did we have a great producer in Perry, who was both soft spoken and firm, but we also had a back room of some of the best writers of the day, including Larry Gelbart, Mel Tolkin, Shelly Keller, Paul Mazursky, Herb Baker, Ernie Chambers, Saul Ilson and Larry Tucker.

Sometimes it seemed like there was almost a dozen of them in the writers' room. I would stop by, fresh off the plane from New York, and poke my head in the door. It would smell like a deli in there, full of pickles and pastrami and corned beef—why did every writer's room have to smell like that?—and they would be throwing jokes around, saying, "Good… Bad… Use it… In… Out… It doesn't work." They would replay the joke again and again in different forms until they either rejected it for good or kept it to be refined later for that week's show. There was such an interaction between all of them, eight guys in a room, reworking jokes one after another.

I loved telling stories and so I would often stop by and tap on the door.

"Hiya, fellas," I'd say. "Boy, have I got a joke for you."

"Oh, the suit's got a joke for us," someone would say. "Hey, everyone stop and listen to what this dumb guy has to say."

I would tell the joke. And there would be silence in the room. Eight blank faces looking at me.

"You finished?" someone would ask.

"Why, yeah," I'd say. Then, after a few seconds of silence, I would leave.

No sooner was the door closed than I would hear howls of laughter. I did not find out until much later that they made a rule—anybody laughs, we'll kill you.

I loved to go down there, the big boss from New York. These guys could not wait to kick the shit out of me. Sometimes there was such laughter when I left the room that it sounded like they were in pain.

One would yell, "You got any more?"

And I would shout back. "Screw all of you. You're a real pain in the ass."

And then someone else would shout, "Who told you to come?"

I do not think I ever got a straight line out of any of them.

One of the most important decisions regarding the buildup to the *Danny Kaye* premiere was where to schedule the show. CBS had two obvious spots open for the 1963-64 season: Sundays at 9 p.m. following *Ed Sullivan*, or Wednesdays at 10 p.m. following *The Beverly Hillbillies* and *The Dick Van Dyke Show*. Now, although the Sunday night slot was the most prestigious hour of television—9 p.m. on the busiest night of the week—it pitted whatever was placed there against one of the biggest shows of the day: NBC's *Bonanza*. Ted Ashley and Danny Kaye very shrewdly pushed for the safer Wednesday night slot, and I gave it to them.

Now, if scheduling had been Danny's biggest demand he may have qualified as one of my less exacting stars. But it quickly turned out that facilities at Television City in Hollywood were far below his expectations.

Danny complained that his dressing room was way too small, not just for him to change between acts but also to accommodate his colleagues and friends who would drop by at all times, day and night. I was stumped. Every inch of Television City was full. There was nowhere to expand even if we wanted to accommodate Danny. Then, some bright guy came up with the idea of a rooftop penthouse. In those days there was never any question of cost. If Danny wanted it, Danny got it. And within a matter of months we constructed a penthouse suite on the roof of Television City, where Danny could entertain and even stay overnight if he had a late finish or an early start. The cost, $75,000, was a small price to pay for a happy star.

Up on the roof Danny was now happy. But in the studio the reality of weekly television could be tough, especially if the numbers were poor. In its

opening weeks, despite weak opposition and tons of publicity, Kaye failed
to break the magic 30-share barrier—one-third of the television audience in
his time period—that guarantees promotion to the following year's schedule.
Nevertheless, throughout that first season, Kaye's numbers climbed slowly. He
was a great talent, and Perry built just the right show around him.

Some people suggested the show suffered because it was scheduled too late
for children. But *The Danny Kaye Show* was not a children's show. Although
Danny had a reputation for being good with kids and had worked with
UNICEF for years, he was never really a children's entertainer and as far I could
tell, he did not really like children all that much. Anyone who had seen Danny
on tour knew that he was an adult performer. In fact, one of his best acts was
simply to sit on the edge of the stage and talk to the audience, a skill which
Perry incorporated into the TV show.

Danny was not a comic in the traditional sense—not a Don Rickles or a
Morey Amsterdam—but he was funny. And boy, could he sing and dance. He
was a big hit. And despite the fact that he never came close to achieving ratings
on the scale of *The Beverly Hillbillies*, he won a lot of awards and he made a lot
of money.

Danny always treated me extremely well. He was a man of many talents and
many hobbies. And as well as being one of the foremost entertainers of his day,
he was also a skilled pilot and an excellent chef. He loved to cook and he would
call me regularly in New York and ask whether I was coming out to the Coast
the following week. If I told him I was coming Sunday he would say, "Why
don't you fly in Saturday and then spend Sunday over at my place. Come for
breakfast and don't eat anything before you arrive."

He lived in a nice-sized house in Beverly Hills that would probably have
seemed enormous to the average American, but compared to his neighbors
it was not too extravagant. I would arrive sometime around 10 and Danny
would say, "I'm going to make something special for breakfast. What do you
feel like?" He had a regular kitchen and he would make me a special kind of an
omelet there and then. After breakfast he would clap his hands and say, "Right,
now what are we going to have for dinner? I'm going to San Francisco to shop.
You're going back to the Beverly Hills Hotel and you will meet me back here
this evening. On no account are you to eat any lunch." And with that, he
would hop in his private plane and fly up to San Francisco to buy the ingredi-
ents in Chinatown.

Special meals at Danny's house were, more often than not, Chinese. It
was his favorite food. I think he even spent some time learning how to cook

Chinese food aboard floating restaurants in Hong Kong. When he visited New York, he would sometimes instruct me to book out a Chinese restaurant for the evening, where he would promptly take over the kitchen and whip up a fantastic meal, all the while entertaining the staff with his limited Cantonese. Danny did not just have hobbies, he really learned things and he threw himself into them. He even had a special Chinese kitchen built outside his house.

Danny's home-cooked dinners were always intimate affairs, involving no more than four or five people. There would be perhaps a writer or a performer, a designer from Paris, a philosopher, or maybe a journalist like Chet Huntley or David Brinkley. Danny also loved to entertain dignitaries, and he would often invite a senator, a governor, or an ambassador. The limit was always between four or five so that we could fit around a circular outdoor table where Danny would cook about a dozen dishes using a variety of woks and pans. Then he would give us all plates—never one for himself—and he would sit next to someone for the meal, usually me when I was there, and eat from their dish.

Flying was perhaps the one thing that Danny was as passionate about as cooking. He had his own private Beechcraft Queen Air plane. I managed to avoid joining Danny on his flights at first; I was terrified of heights and too scared to go up in such a small plane. But eventually I had to give in. He once flew me to Las Vegas to see Sinatra perform. The Beechcraft Queen Air is a twin-engine plane, and I was terrified something might go wrong and we would crash in the middle of the desert. But I could not easily pass up the chance of a special concert with Sinatra. The flight took about an hour and a half. We saw Sinatra perform and then went with him to a private restaurant for a late-night meal and stayed overnight before flying back to L.A. in the morning.

There was a lot of talk in those days that Danny might have been homosexual, or at least bisexual. I never saw any evidence of it, though I know he spent an awful lot of time with Cary Grant and Laurence Olivier. Danny was a very private person, not much of a socialite, and very discerning about the people he mixed with. The rumors were always in the back of my mind when I visited but I never saw any evidence they were true, though there was one incident at Danny's place that left me feeling a little uncomfortable.

I suffered with back problems for many years. My right hip would go into spasms very often because of the fact that one leg was shorter than the other from my polio. Regular transcontinental flights did little to ease the pain, and I eventually had to seek the help of Dr. Hans Kraus, the top back doctor of the day who also treated President Kennedy. Dr. Kraus showed me a number of exercises I could do on the floor to ease the pain. And on this particular occasion at Danny's as soon as the pain struck I yelped and dropped to the floor, lifting my knees up towards my chest and holding them there to ease the tension in my lower back. As the pain subsided I opened my eyes to see Cary Grant and Danny Kaye both looking down at me in an uncomfortable sort of way. I smiled sheepishly and there was an awkward silence before the conversation resumed. Maybe I imagined it, I don't know. But it did remain a good after-dinner tale for decades to come.

Either way, Danny was a gentleman and his show was a great success. Scheduling Judy Garland, on the other hand, proved to be one of the most ill-fated, and traumatic, decisions of my career.

II.

The End of the Rainbow

"All in all the show was a good thing to have happened to me. I learned a great deal. But if I had known what I was in for, I would never have tried a weekly series. Not ever." – Judy Garland, 1964, quoted in *Rainbow's End: The Judy Garland Show*.

Though Danny Kaye was always very welcoming towards me, there was one occasion when he lost his temper completely, and that was over Judy Garland. Both stars debuted in the same week in the fall of 1963, and I had slotted Judy into the Sunday night prime-time period left when Danny opted for Wednesday evenings at 10 p.m. Since their shows opened the same week, Danny invited Judy and me, and a couple of friends, to his home to watch the premiere of *The Judy Garland Show*. After a delicious meal we retired to the sofa to watch the broadcast at 9 o'clock.

Although we were about to watch the first of Judy's forthcoming 32-episode series, Judy had already endured a tumultuous start during the prerecording of almost a dozen shows. There had been a number of clashes with the network, and her first producer, George Schlatter, had recently been fired by CBS, largely because of a difference of opinion with our West Coast vice president, Hunt Stromberg. Judy's debut preceded months of speculation that the highly strung and insecure star would not have the stamina for weekly television.

The premiere opened with Judy singing "Call Me Irresponsible," which was supposed to be a dig at naysayers in the press. She had been suffering from laryngitis, and it sometimes showed through in her voice. Nevertheless, the show was not bad. And throughout the next 60 minutes, I would pass the occasional comment on how marvelous Judy looked and how wonderful the show seemed to be going. Danny, on the other hand, sat in total silence. When the credits rolled, he turned to me and said, "Could I see you for a moment in my bedroom?"

I followed Danny upstairs and into his room where he told me to sit on his bed.

"How could you do that to that woman?" he said.

"What do you mean, Danny?"

"You have destroyed her."

"What do you mean I have destroyed her?"

"You've destroyed her career. I was ashamed to watch that show. It's awful, and Judy looks terrible. Terrible."

Danny berated me for the next five minutes while I tried to defend myself, saying that I thought the show was wonderful and that Judy came across very well indeed. But Danny would not listen. He was going crazy and he really let me have it.

When he was done, he ordered me out of the bedroom and back downstairs. I walked into the lounge feeling awful for poor Judy, who had had to sit there all this time. She was looking at me as if she could not understand what could possibly be going on.

"Hi, everybody," I said. "What a thing, what a thing." And went over and kissed her and told her again how marvelous she had been.

We received some letters of concern from a handful of fans after that show but also a lot of fan mail. And I never forgave Danny for being so harsh in front of Judy. She was a fragile person, and however much he cared about her and her career, I thought it was a very mean thing to do.

On the other hand, Danny's concern was not misplaced. Over the coming months, what started out as an unsteady premiere quickly descended into a fiasco.

The Judy Garland Show had begun promisingly with a call from Judy's manager, David Begelman, saying she wanted a shot at weekly television. Like Danny Kaye, Judy was no stranger to the small screen. In fact, her 1962 TV special, produced by Norman Jewison, had been a critical as well as a ratings success. When David explained that Judy felt she could replicate that quality in a weekly format, I was thrilled.

David was a very heavy hitter. He and Freddie Fields, both former executives at MCA, had founded their own agency called Creative Management Associates, or CMA. They brought a lot of street smarts to the industry. And they were both very naughty boys, not the kind of people you would want looking after your affairs. But, then again, a lot of the agents were moochers. If a star got a free television set, his agent got a free television set. If a celebrity got a free car, his agent got a free car. The only difference with David and Freddie was that often the star never knew they had a television set or a car coming to them. Later, David got into a lot of trouble for allegedly stealing money from his clients, and he shot himself in a Los Angeles hotel room. But whatever his faults, he was a fun guy to be around and I loved to hear from him. He was such a bright man and very funny. So when he contacted me about the possibility of Judy returning to television with her own show, I was delighted.

"Mike, Judy needs money," David said. "And I want her to do some shows for you."

What could I say? "Well, Jesus, David, how much does she want?"

It turned out that Judy's return to network television would cost CBS $150,000 per show. Judy's company, Kingsrow Enterprises, would produce the program, and Judy was set to walk away with $25,000 per episode. Since we were still struggling to dislodge *Bonanza* in that Sunday evening time slot, and since Aubrey's picks of *The Real McCoys* and *G.E. True* the previous season had failed miserably, I figured a musical-variety show starring Judy Garland was worth the gamble. If the show worked, it would dislodge our main competitor. And if it failed, Judy always had the excuse that she was going head-to-head with one of the top shows in television.

By the time I got to know Judy she was in the process of divorcing her third husband and former manager, Sid Luft, and she had mounting financial worries. She was warm and charming, yet there was a sadness and a fragility to her. Only a few years earlier she had been hospitalized after losing 60 pounds on a crash diet because she was so overweight.

Judy was a very sad person. I remember once, after a big concert she gave in New York, I accompanied her to her hotel. She had an enormous suite—it must have had about a dozen rooms, including an elegant dining room and a living room with a piano. We were the only two people there. She poured herself a glass of Liebfraumilch, sat down next to me and said, "You know, this happens all the time, Mike. I come from these crowds and the noise and everything else and suddenly I'm alone. It's a terrible feeling, isn't it?"

There was no doubt that Judy was a depressive. But her suffering was compounded by a dependency on pills that had started in early childhood. She told me once that as a child star at MGM with Mickey Rooney they had been given pills regularly, uppers in the morning to stimulate them for the day ahead, and downers at night to make them go to sleep.

After signing Judy we brought in George Schlatter, a talented producer, to run the show. Our biggest concern was that Judy might not make rehearsals on time, if at all. So, even though Judy had recently bought a house in Brentwood, Schlatter pleaded with us to provide some sort of incentive, similar to Danny Kaye's penthouse, to ensure Judy turned up for work each day. The result was a 400-square-foot trailer, parked near Studio 43 where *The Judy Garland Show* was performed.

Of course, Judy Garland's trailer was a trailer like no other. Topped with a red and white canvas roof and surrounded by artificial grass, it was reached via a yellow brick road leading up a ramp to the front door. Inside were a handful of wonderful rooms: a kitchen, a bar, and a carpeted living and dining area with pink lighting. The entire thing must have cost about $150,000. But it was worth it because from the outset Judy seemed balanced and happy, and it looked as though our gamble was going to pay off. But the project soon ran into difficulties. Chief among these was the meddling of Hunt Stromberg and Jim Aubrey.

Aubrey and Stromberg were antagonistic towards Judy from the start, thanks no doubt in part to the fact that Judy's biggest booster at CBS was Hubbell Robinson.

Paley had reinstated Hubbell in 1962, much to Aubrey's displeasure, in the hopes of resurrecting some of the quality that had marked the height of the "Tiffany Network." But Hubbell's days at CBS were numbered from the moment he arrived, and Aubrey did all he could to get rid of him. In March 1963, one year after rejoining the company, Aubrey called Hubbell into his office to chew him out about something. Hubbell spent a half hour explaining the situation to Aubrey. But when he was finished Aubrey still had a number of concerns.

"I can explain those too," Hubbell said.

"That isn't necessary, you're through," Aubrey replied.

Hubbell thought Aubrey meant he was through explaining. But unbeknown to Hubbell, Aubrey had already arranged for his "resignation" from CBS. With Hubbell gone, it was time for Aubrey and Stromberg to sink their teeth into Judy.

To be sure, there was something about Judy's performance, a nervousness perhaps, that showed through in the television broadcast. She was not as natural a television star as Danny Kaye, and the program suffered from some poor writing and execution. But it was nowhere near the disaster that Aubrey and Stromberg perceived it to be.

Nevertheless, Aubrey and Stromberg pushed on. They focused on George Schlatter, deciding that he was giving CBS the wrong kind of show, that he had put Judy on a pedestal where she was unreachable for the masses who preferred the quaint charms of *The Beverly Hillbillies* and *Bonanza*. Aubrey and Stromberg wanted to make Judy more folksy, to bring her down a peg or two, to humanize her for the mass audience. So they started applying pressure to Schlatter to insert a bit more self-deprecating humor into the program to show

Judy's human side. Schlatter took a stand. He refused to cave to Aubrey and Stromberg. And after less than a half-dozen shows they fired him and brought in Norman Jewison to give the show some of the folksiness they felt it deserved.

Stromberg was a truly horrible man, untrustworthy, cruel and more vindictive than Aubrey, though far less intelligent. He was truly hated by many of the stars, and he may have been the most reviled man at CBS at the time, which was saying something considering it was during the reign of the Smiling Cobra. For reasons I will never know, he kept a pet monkey in his office. And he seemed to particularly enjoy sticking his nose into programs, baiting producers and stars.

Without an agent the caliber of Ted Ashley looking out for Judy, she was vulnerable to Stromberg's incessant and demeaning visits to the studio, where he would tell Judy how to make herself more likable to the people at home. Although Judy stood her ground—she is rumored to have said, "Fuck you, Hunt" during one particularly heated meeting—away from the negotiating table I am sure the pressure took its toll.

Meanwhile, when Aubrey flew in from the East Coast he would make sure to pay Judy a visit and wear her down a little more. Aubrey never got involved in a production unless he wanted to attack it. And he went after Judy in all manner of ways: bad mouthing her around the office, constantly pressuring her to make herself more down-to-earth.

The fact of the matter was that singers very rarely make a successful transition into weekly television. Frank Sinatra had failed three times—and Sinatra was not up against *Bonanza*. What chance did Judy stand? She sang very well and she had some of the best people on her show. But she was under pressure from all sides: CBS, her personal life, her finances.

The press, always looking for a juicy story, began to report on the behind-the-scenes turmoil, and Judy wobbled. By the end of August, a few weeks ahead of the show's premiere, she checked herself into hospital for a couple of days suffering from stress. When the first show aired, the critics gave Judy the benefit of the doubt. But as the season progressed her numbers declined, as did Judy's reliability. She began to turn up late for rehearsals. Sometimes she did not turn up at all. And there were occasions when, suffering from a lack of sleep or perhaps one too many glasses of Liebfraumilch, she would fluff her lines. Rehearsals could often run into the early hours of the morning and beyond.

Yet, despite the pressure from Aubrey and Stromberg, Judy was always very gracious to me. She treated me like a father figure and often turned to me for company and for advice. She hated to be on her own, and it was standard practice for anyone working with her in those days to receive invitations to her house or telephone calls in the middle of the night. If I was in Hollywood, we would often eat together at La Scala until 2 or 3 in the morning, and I would accompany her home. When I was in Chappaqua I used to get calls at 3 in the morning from Judy panicking, saying things like, "They're coming over the walls, Mike. They're coming over the walls."

My wife was going crazy with suspicion. But despite the fact that Judy had affairs with very many men, I can safely say that I was one of the few she found sufficiently unattractive to pursue.

Judy was talented. Her show had some marvelous high points, including wonderful performances not just by Judy but also duets with a very young Barbra Streisand and a feisty Ethel Merman. But she was also terribly insecure. As the poor numbers continued to come in, adding to her stresses over mounting personal and financial problems, I was constantly worried I would get a phone call saying Judy had quit, or gone crazy, or worse.

My fears were confirmed when I received a call at the Beverly Hills Hotel from David Begelman late one morning,

"We have a very big problem, Mike."

"Oh, God," I said.

"You'd better come down and solve it cause she's really—I think she's going to kill herself."

I was worried sick. "What can I do?"

"She says she wants to see you alone in her trailer."

I seriously considered taking a security guard in there with me, just in case Judy blamed me for the bad publicity. But I decided against it. Since Judy had always relied on me, I thought, she would not want to harm me.

When I entered the trailer Judy was standing in a full black-and-white striped convict outfit topped off with a black-and-white striped hat. She motioned for me to sit down, set some music playing and then performed one of her song-and-dance routines. I did not know whether to laugh or cry. David and Judy thought it was terribly funny, but I was a nervous wreck.

As the ratings continued to decline and the pressure increased, Judy became even more erratic. Norman had to leave the project at the end of October because of a prior engagement producing Rock Hudson and Doris Day in *Send Me No Flowers*. Judy pushed for CBS to reinstate Schlatter, but Aubrey and Stromberg were adamant.

By now, I was convinced they wanted Judy's show to fail. It was a typical Aubrey power play. He simply did not like the woman, and he was going to make sure she went down. *Bonanza* was killing Judy. But although we could have moved her to a different time period, Aubrey refused. Likewise, he refused to allow Schlatter to return to the show. Instead, we brought in Bill Colleran for the final episodes of Judy's first season.

It is possible, though, that Judy was beyond saving. Not only was the show doing badly but her personal affairs seemed to fall apart in front of our eyes. Allegations surfaced that David Begelman had embezzled tens of thousands of dollars from Judy. And her husband Sid started custody proceedings over their two children. She was perhaps, in a tragic respect, our own Edith Piaf.

As the weeks went on it became apparent that Judy was taking more pills and having trouble sleeping. Her performances were erratic. Worse still, the pressure started to show. On television, it was not just her voice that suffered; even her face looked worn. When the cameras moved in for their close-up, they were very unkind. Judy was only 4 foot 11 inches. And now, in front of a nation, she appeared like a tired, fragile woman, older than her 41 years.

When Judy sang in nightclubs or in the movies, the audience had no inkling of the physical toll her personal suffering took. But the television cameras did not lie. I got angry letters from fans asking how I could treat her in such a way. But there was nothing I could do. By the beginning of 1964 it was obvious that Judy's show was not going to be renewed. And, sure enough, in the middle of January, Aubrey pulled the plug.

CBS allowed Judy to save face by writing a public letter of resignation to the network, citing the need to spend more time with her children as her major reason for pulling out. But everyone knew the truth. Aubrey had crushed her. And I am sure it is no coincidence that years later, when he took over MGM, he sold the red slippers she had worn in the *Wizard of Oz* to raise capital.

But despicable as they were, Aubrey and Stromberg were not ultimately to blame for Judy's downfall. Judy could do anything. She could sing, she could dance, she could act. She was a real trooper, possibly the greatest single virtuoso female performer in the business. But such traits do not guarantee television success. The greatest stars have flopped on television. Mediocrity often reigns. *Bonanza* was big in Buffalo and big in Wyoming. It was even big in New York City, once it got going. But you could not say the same for Judy. Would she have done better in another time period? Possibly. We certainly put her in a death trap. But at the end of the day the show was beyond saving for a number of reasons, a mixture of bad timing and bad luck as well as Judy's fragility and her unsuitability for the rigors of weekly television.

Countless people tried to save Judy's show—producers, writers, directors, guest stars. Yet it could not be saved. Even today, I am sure there are still people who think they know how it could have been salvaged. But I knew then that the close-up of the camera was the harshest critic. It showed the skin and bones, the thinness, the fragility and the sorrow.

As if to add insult to injury, Judy Garland was replaced in the 1964 schedule by a couple of second-rate half-hour sitcoms, *My Living Doll* and *The Joey Bishop Show*. I took it as a mark of respect that Judy maintained her relationship with me even after the cancellation of the show. She knew I had done whatever I could to help her, even though the forces of Aubrey and Stromberg were incredibly strong.

But going into the 1964-65 season I had problems of my own. Throughout the past couple of years, Aubrey's behavior had become more and more questionable. He started approving business deals that seemed to be going against the best interests of the network, deals that I was becoming increasingly uncomfortable with. Aubrey knew I was not loyal to him. And that meant that after dispatching Hubbell Robinson and Judy Garland, I was now nearing the top of his list of people to remove from the CBS payroll.

12.

Wrestling the Cobra

"I don't pretend to be any saint. If anyone wants to indict me for liking pretty girls, I'm guilty." – Jim Aubrey, "How Now, Dick Daring?" The New York Times, September 10, 1972.

The television industry has always involved backstabbing and infighting. It was an insecure industry then and it is an insecure industry now. The only difference is that the money has more zeroes on the end of it. During the 1963-64 season, CBS had nine of the top 10 prime-time shows and nine of the top 10 daytime shows. We were at the top of our game. Yet life at the network was hell. Aubrey ruled with a steely determination and arrogance, continuing to alienate stars and producers with his blunt rejections and put-downs. Hunt Stromberg Jr., who was supposed to report to me, had a direct line to the president's office and regularly went behind my back to Aubrey. With the exception of Stromberg and a few other Aubrey "yes" men, morale at the network was terribly low.

I had a number of allies. For a start, I was still an asset in Paley's eyes. I was also good friends with Jerry Leider, in charge of specials, and Sal Ianucci in our legal department. In April of 1963, I hired another executive, Fred Silverman, to join our program department. At 25, Fred was one of the youngest executives of his day. He had been recommended as something of a college whiz kid, and I put him in charge of daytime programming. In no time, Fred built the first successful Saturday morning schedule in CBS history. But it was quite a tense atmosphere for someone so young. It was probably only in his second month when he came into my office nervous about a presentation he had to give to Paley, Stanton and Aubrey.

"Don't worry about it, kid," I said. "Why don't you practice on me now?"

Fred sat facing the window while I closed the door. Since the rehearsal was going to take some time I decided to lie down on the couch. Fred delivered his presentation, haltingly at first and soon settling into a nice rhythm. I do not know how long he took, but I do know that he had to shake me quite violently to get me to wake up.

"Look, kid, you'll do just fine anyway," I said. And he did.

In fact, presentations in front of the boss were one of the safest arenas in which to face the Smiling Cobra. Aubrey never enjoyed anything that did not involve sleight of hand, and the chop was always going to come from somewhere out of left field.

Working under such a president meant that my daily focus began to shift from programming to pleasing Aubrey. Missions included calling David Susskind to arrange a part in a show for a girl that Aubrey was sleeping with or dashing outside at Aubrey's request to see if his car and driver had arrived. I started taking pills to sleep at night.

It was around this time that John Mitchell, of the television company Screen Gems, brought me the pilot for a new show called *Bewitched*, starring Robert Montgomery's daughter, Elizabeth. I thought the show was marvelous. By now, Paley was barely taking an interest in programming, but I sent the pilot to his home nevertheless, knowing that he would appreciate it. Paley loved the show. And by the time I brought it to Aubrey, I was confident he would give it his blessing because another situation comedy would fit neatly into his programming strategy.

I attended the screening with Aubrey and John Mitchell and I was not disappointed when, after the lights went up, Aubrey issued his trademark "not bad" response, which meant that Aubrey liked it too. I thought we had the whole thing wrapped up until Mitchell turned to Aubrey and said that he had one stipulation—if CBS bought the show it would have to agree to Ralston Purina as a co-sponsor because Mitchell had already guaranteed them half the program.

"Sorry," Aubrey said, without a hint of emotion. "That's not going to happen."

"But I told Ralston Purina they could have half of it before I came to Mike with the show," Mitchell said. "I gave them my word."

Jim looked straight at John, with cold, blue eyes and calmly and quietly commanded, "I'll determine who's on a show I've bought. And I don't want Ralston Purina."

"Well, there's nothing I can do."

"Okay," Aubrey said, his voice barely a whisper. "Then get out of my office."

When Mitchell left, Aubrey was livid. "I don't give a shit what that S.O.B. agreed," he said. "Nobody presents a show to me and tells me they have a sponsor for half of it. If I buy the show, I buy the show. It's *my* show."

A few days later Mitchell met with ABC and sold *Bewitched* without any fuss. The third-placed network was only too happy to take it. They put it on Thursday nights at 9 p.m. and it was a big hit, a show that we really could have done with for the forthcoming 1964-65 season. But that did not sway Aubrey one bit. He wanted total control.

There was more to Aubrey's temper than just ego and hubris. There was greed too. For as I already knew very well, though Aubrey refused to cozy up to stars, station affiliates and even Paley, he had a very close relationship with producers, especially Marty Ransohoff of Filmways and Keefe Brasselle of Richelieu Productions.

The relationship with Ransohoff I could understand. Ransohoff had brought CBS *The Beverly Hillbillies* in 1962. But Keefe Brasselle was a mystery.

Brasselle was a second-rate song-and-dance man whose starring role in *The Eddie Cantor Story* in 1953 had been the sole highlight of an otherwise mediocre career. But he and Aubrey went way back. They had known each other since Aubrey's days on the West Coast as a salesman for CBS, when Brasselle had been a rising star. And now they were closer than Aubrey was to most of his colleagues at 485 Madison. By the 1960s, Brasselle was running Richelieu Productions out of offices at CBS's broadcast facility at 57th Street.

Brasselle was slick, handsome, possibly even better looking than Aubrey, and more menacing too. He was married to an Italian singer, Arlene DeMarco of the DeMarco sisters, and he always hinted at ties to the mob. When Brasselle opened a New Jersey nightclub in 1960, Aubrey sent a memo ordering CBS executives to take their wives. Joanne hated television functions, so there was no way I was going to persuade her to travel to some lousy flea pit in Jersey. Much to Aubrey's displeasure, I was the only employee who disobeyed orders. But I was relieved the next morning, when I heard from colleagues that walking into Brasselle's "Hollywood Club" was like entering a scene from *The Godfather*, with all of the men sat at one table and the wives at another. The club did very poorly and burned down in an arson attack the following year.

Although Brasselle was not as physically imposing as Aubrey, he carried himself like a gangster and he was therefore much more intimidating. Many years later, I heard that he was arrested for shooting a man in a barroom brawl. When Brasselle asked for a favor, I was never quite sure whether it was a request or an order. And since he was best pals with Aubrey, I pretty much did as I was told. He used to hang his suits in the wardrobe in my office and he would pop in now and again to get changed on his way to a fancy lunch with a star.

I do not think anyone ever got to the bottom of the ties between Aubrey and Brasselle. But in the spring of 1964, a scandal sheet called *Hollywood Close-up* started printing stories questioning Aubrey's integrity. Among the accusations were charges that Aubrey was using a car and driver supplied by Richelieu Productions and an apartment on Central Park South subsidized by Filmways.

The allegations seemed ludicrous if for no other reason than Jim already had a car and driver provided by CBS. And if he wanted an apartment, the company could have provided one of those too. But Aubrey was leading a double life in those days. And it was just possible that he wanted to keep some of his darker interests, especially his romantic adventures, at arm's length from CBS.

Aubrey's sexual prowess was legendary. He had numerous affairs and finally divorced his wife, Phyllis Thaxter, in 1962. His dashing looks and perfect physique meant that he never had trouble finding women. But there were persistent rumors that Brasselle also procured girls for him in New York and Vegas, while Hunt Stromberg, Jr., who was homosexual, would procure girls, and possibly even boys, when he was in L.A.

There were also whispers around the office that Aubrey was far from a gentleman; rumors hinted that he could be violent and that on more than one occasion a liaison with Aubrey culminated in a trip to the hospital. When a young Sherry Lansing, later to become the CEO of Paramount, ended up on crutches for 18 months after being sideswiped by a car while out with Aubrey in the 1970s, the joke in the corridors of Madison Avenue was that she was lucky she never made it home with him.

Sex was an extension of power for Aubrey. And he wielded it as he wielded everything else. Despite his run-ins with Judy Garland, he still managed to add her to his many conquests. She was weak and malleable and attracted to alpha types. As if to prove a point, if the rumors were true, Aubrey had his way with her in his office at CBS with the door slightly ajar so that he could show the producer David Susskind what a big man he was.

My strategy of keeping the beast at arm's length came to an abrupt halt during the summer of 1964 when our legal counsel Sal Ianucci brought me a memo transferring the ownership of two shows, *The Baileys of Balboa* and *The Cara Williams Show*, from CBS to Brasselle's Richelieu Productions. As far as I could work out, the deal would net Brasselle at least a quarter of a million dollars if the shows did not go on the air and considerably more if they did. When I asked Sal why the shows were being transferred, his answer was simply, "The boss wants it."

I went to pieces. If I let the memo pass without taking any action, I would be complicit in what I believed to be an illegal deal. But if I did take action, it would be tantamount to picking a fight with Aubrey and Brasselle. I decided to turn to Frank Stanton.

In Stanton's office I explained the entire story as a "hypothetical," with my ultimate question being whether or not I should use my own leverage as vice president, programming, to call off the deal, or whether I should proceed and give up part of our company's capital possessions. Stanton, normally so precise, spoke guardedly. He said that every situation is new and that under such circumstances I would have to make up my own mind. However, he added, he was sure that if such a situation was to arise then the most senior managers would be compelled to step in. At that moment, I knew that Stanton and Paley would make sure the deal was never finalized. Stanton said that he would have CBS's chief counsel, Ralph Colin, investigate.

I felt reassured. I knew that Colin was a top lawyer who had been with Paley longer than almost anybody else. He would find out immediately if it was a rotten deal. When Colin returned we had a meeting in my office where he told me that everything was in hand. I remember I got very excited and kept saying, "That's just great."

But when Colin said, "We've got it worked out," I took it to mean that Keefe Brasselle would be barred from the lots and Aubrey would be dismissed. However, no action was taken. It was very upsetting. And I could not figure out how Stanton, with Paley's blessing no doubt, could whitewash over the whole thing. That summer and into the fall, I would go home at 7 or 8 o'clock each night with two things on my mind: how to please Aubrey and how to get Aubrey.

The fall schedule opened with three of Brasselle's shows in prime time, two half-hour situation comedies, *The Cara Williams Show* at 9:30 p.m. on Wednesday and *The Baileys of Balboa* at 9:30 p.m. on Thursday. Meanwhile, an hour-long series called *The Reporter* went out at 10 p.m. on Friday. But the Cobra had lost his touch. In the opening weeks of the 1964-65 season, CBS's ratings share plummeted by about 11 percent, and we were challenged aggressively by both NBC and ABC.

By October, Aubrey, Paley and Stanton were beginning to panic. In the middle of the month, Paley gave me permission to temporarily suspend filming three of our new shows, including Brasselle's *The Reporter*. I would have liked to have thrown all of his programs off the air, but just getting shot of one was enough. That evening I took a small group of my boys to Christ Cella restaurant to celebrate when the maître d' came over with a note. It was from Keefe

Brasselle and it simply said: "I will remember this. Keefe." I thought he was going to kill me.

By December, the ratings had barely improved. Rumors began to circulate that Aubrey's position at CBS was in doubt. I went to see Frank Stanton again, this time over a laundry bill for $20,000 for *The Cara Williams Show*. I refused to sign off on it and confronted Stanton.

"Dr. Stanton, I came up here four months ago and I told you that things were going on in the program department that had to be investigated and you never answered back," I said. "I will be interrogated legally at some point, or I fear I will be, and I know this could bring disgrace on my family and my career. I must have you do something."

Again, Stanton said he would look into it, and refused to discuss the matter further.

In mid-December, with NBC and ABC still challenging CBS in the ratings, Aubrey was forced to rejig the schedule. He left the nuts and bolts of the programming moves up to me, and I shifted maybe a dozen shows, including moving *Slattery's People* into the hole where Brasselle's *The Reporter* had been.

By now, Aubrey was out for revenge, and I considered myself the principal target. The word on Madison Avenue was that Aubrey would fire me the first chance he got. David Susskind said he had heard it, Marty Ransohoff said he had heard it, Ted Ashley said he had heard it. I even bumped into a major producer on a plane who said he had heard the same thing.

"I hear you're in trouble and you're going to be fired," he said. "If you stay and Aubrey goes, I'll give you the same deal I gave Jim—in a Swiss bank account too."

Naturally, I went back to Stanton with this information as well. Though no one ever came back to me with any answers.

It was a bleak, nerve-wracking Christmas not knowing how or when Aubrey would get rid of me. The only thing that stopped him from being able to give me the push was the fact that with the ratings slipping and the rumors swirling, his power base had been significantly weakened. Paley appeared to have woken up to his network again. And I felt as though he was keeping a watchful eye on Aubrey's next move from a distance. In January we flew out to Hollywood to finalize the schedule for the 1965 season.

At the meeting Aubrey acted as though his tenure was never in doubt. He presented the 1965 schedule to Paley with his usual swagger. If Aubrey is this confident, I thought, my time is almost up.

By February I was too nervous to go into the office and too afraid to spend time at home in case my wife started asking questions. So I ran away. I told my wife there was an urgent problem I needed to sort out in Hollywood, I flew to California and I hid out at Ted Ashley's house. After a couple of days the phone rang. It was Aubrey looking for me.

Ted took the call in his billiard room but I could hear his half of the conversation clearly.

"I don't know where he is, Jim," I heard Ted say. "I'd like to know, I want to talk to him myself, but I haven't heard from him for a few days now. Is something wrong?… If I see him, I'll be sure to tell him."

When Ted appeared in the living room, he had a thin smile on his face.

"Jim says that as soon as he finds that S.O.B., he is going to kill him."

I gave my career 3:1 odds of not lasting more than another couple of weeks. And if I was not going to be fired, I felt certain that I would be forced out of the company under the most questionable of circumstances. Finally, I went back to New York and waited for Aubrey's call. It came my first day back at the office, asking for a meeting in the Indian restaurant at the Pierre Hotel. I never really liked Indian food that much anyway.

At the Pierre I could feel my arms and legs shaking. I felt sure that this was the place where Aubrey was going to take me out. I was a married man with a wife and three kids, and I was about to get fired by the president of the network. But to my surprise, Aubrey was all smiles.

"I don't know why we can't be friends," he said. "I like you. You like me. We can work this out, kid."

He was a different man. He said that I had some behavioral issues that I needed to fix. But if I quit doing this and that, and just listened to him, he saw no reason why we could not continue our relationship on a professional basis. I could not understand it.

"Pal," he ended the meeting. "I think you and I are going to get along just fine."

I went back to my office wondering what the hell was going on. Aubrey was obviously intent on keeping me. But I had no idea why or for how long. I was like a bouncing ball. I slumped into my chair.

Later that week, Aubrey flew to Miami for a big 49th birthday party at Jackie Gleason's place. He had invited me to come along but at the last minute told me to stay in New York.

On the Friday evening I got a call from Paley, whom I had not heard from for about six months.

"Mr. Paley, how are you?"

"I'm fine. I just called to ask you a question. Is there anything you are worried about in next season's schedule?"

"Well, Mr. Paley, we have a new show from CMA starring Freddie Fields' wife, Polly Bergen. They don't have a pilot for it yet, just a presentation. But I've seen it and I don't think it's very good. Jim wants it for nine thirty on Monday but I'm very worried about it."

"Can't you get another show?"

"ABC has just cancelled a very good show with Shirley Booth about a housekeeper called Hazel. I think that would work very nicely."

"Well, then, put *Hazel* in," Paley said, and rang off.

About a half hour later I got a call from Aubrey.

"How's it going, kid?"

Such warmth I had never experienced in all my life.

"Paley's been on the phone. He's worried about the Polly Bergen show. He's thinking of dropping it for next season."

"Hell, no," Aubrey said. "I don't want to upset Freddie Fields. Don't worry about it, kid. You can ignore the old man. I'll be back in the morning."

The ping pong was back.

Saturday morning I got a call from Frank Stanton. I remember I was still in my pajamas.

"Mike, Mr. Paley has hurt his back and he's in the St. Regis Hotel. We're having a meeting there this afternoon and we would like you to come along. John Reynolds has flown in from the West Coast. We have just accepted the resignation of Jim Aubrey."

I called Ted Ashley.

"I know," Ted said. "It's all over the street. They're bringing in Jack Schneider to take over as president. Aubrey is out."

At the St. Regis Hotel, Mr. Paley was laid on his back and obviously in some pain. He officially informed us that Jim Aubrey had handed in his resignation and that Jack Schneider would be taking over as president. Then he turned to me and said, "What are you going to do about the West Coast?"—meaning, what was I going to do about Stromberg and his cronies.

"Probably change it," I said.

"Good," said Paley. "And since Aubrey resigned and since you seem to know so much about programming, I suppose the program department is now your total responsibility."

Suddenly, I went from a guy who was running for his life to a guy who was running the program department of the highest-rated network in America. I had an annual programming budget of almost $400 million. And with only three major networks in competition in 1965, being head of CBS' programming department then gave me more influence than all the heads of the networks today combined. My title carried enormous power. And over the next few years I exercised it constantly.

But I never did find out the precise reason why Aubrey was fired. There were rumors about an incident at the party in Miami when cops had to be called, or rumors that Aubrey's behavior became intolerable once the ratings started to decline. Other people said Aubrey had conspired with a bunch of investors to take over CBS and kick Paley out. But no one ever found a single, concrete reason for his "resignation."

Many years later, after both Stanton and I had left CBS, I called Frank specifically to find out the answer to this question that had nagged at me for years. I invited him to The Four Seasons and, over lunch, I asked him in various ways what had prompted the dismissal. But although Stanton was gracious and cordial, he refused to answer.

"That's an interesting question, Mike," he would say, and then continue with his meal. The three men who knew the answer to that question—Paley, Stanton and Aubrey—are all dead now. I guess there are some things that people will never know.

13.

Free at Last

"There is no such thing as quality and taste with no audience."
– William S. Paley, 1961.

The first action I took after being promoted to head of programming was to fly to the West Coast and fire Hunt Stromberg and almost his entire staff. Stromberg must have known it was coming; there was no love lost between us. Within a short time both he and Aubrey set up a Hollywood production firm called The Aubrey Company. But I did not care what they did, as long as they were out of CBS.

Paley made sure that a CBS president would never again be able to exert such control over the network. Aubrey's replacement, Jack Schneider, the former general manager of WCBS-TV, was a nice enough guy but he was nothing compared to the Pat Weavers, or even the Bob Kintners, of the television world. Schneider could talk on any subject for one minute. But that was about the best that you could say about him. I may have been a vice president, but the unspoken truth was that I had much more power than Schneider.

My first concern was building a program team on the West Coast, where Stromberg had run Television City into the ground. He had surrounded himself with yes men, many of whom had little or no prior experience in the entertainment industry. And for the few talented individuals who had sneaked in through the cracks, it must have been quite an ordeal working for such a boss. The only members of Stromberg's staff whom I kept on in the office were Ethel Winant, a wonderful script editor who later became one of the first female network executives in America, and Angela Lansbury's son Bruce, a marvelous TV producer. Everyone else had to go.

The West Coast was by now the undisputed center of television production. It was where CBS's schedule lived and died. And though I may have been a good marketer, and even a good critic, I knew my limitations. Working as a comedy scriptwriter for Jack Albertson 20 years earlier had taught me that I was not a creative man. If our program department was going to stay ahead in the ratings, Television City would have to be staffed with the best creative team of the day.

Heading up this new team would be no simple task. It required an encyclopedic knowledge of the industry and the experience to be able to manage the most demanding stars, agents and advertisers, not to mention the needs and desires of both myself and Bill Paley. Since most CBS employees had been tainted one way or another by the double dealing, threats and intimidation of the Aubrey years, I cast my net as wide as possible. I could think of no one at the other networks who was both sufficiently talented and looking for work, so I widened my search until one day it hit me that the answer had been right under my nose: Perry Lafferty.

Admittedly, it was slightly unusual in the 1960s to hire a producer-director for such a senior network position. But Lafferty had proven himself both a creative master and more than capable of handling stars. A network vice presidency seemed a logical step. However, Perry took some persuading. He had had a rough time dealing with CBS in recent years, particularly with Hunt Stromberg, who had tried to have him fired from *The Danny Kaye Show*. It was a leap of faith for Perry to make the switch to the network side of the industry, so I offered him a starting salary of $150,000—which was $25,000 more than I was then earning—if he would take the chance. Jack Schneider thought I was crazy.

"Why in the hell are you paying him more than you're getting paid?"

"Because he's the best," I said. "And because if he turns out to be good, he'll save me millions."

Indeed, Perry turned out to be critical to my success over the coming years. He contributed to almost every one of our hits. Not only that, but he put together a great West Coast team, with experts in comedy, drama, variety and specials. Certainly, there were elements of the programming field that Perry still had to learn, but that was only to be expected.

One of Perry's first lessons was the need to separate personal preferences from programming decisions. During his first couple of months, he pronounced the pilot for a show called *The Trials of O'Brien* one of the best programs he had seen in ages and remarked that we would be fools not to sign it.

"Just a second, Perry," I said. "The first rule of programming is to remember that what *you* think is not nearly as important as what the *viewer* thinks. You may believe this show is going to be a great success, but I can tell you now the audience is not going to like it."

Sure enough, *The Trials of O'Brien* tested poorly in focus groups and flopped on television. But Perry never repeated the same mistake twice. He was the consummate programming professional.

More importantly, from a personal point of view, Perry was one of the few people who knew how to handle me. He knew when to listen and when to tell me to shut up. And he was not afraid to call me out if I was being a pain in the ass.

Soon after Perry assembled his new staff, I flew out to the West Coast to welcome everyone and to give them a little pep talk. It was well known that Stromberg had given jobs to inexperienced and under-qualified men, particularly young, pretty ones who were Stromberg's favorites. So I began the meeting by outlining the previous few years of incompetence—and terror—and by saying that the days of personal favors and favoritism were over. Never again would anyone who was not a producer, a writer or a director work in this office. And never again would a CBS employee have to work in an atmosphere of fear.

"We'll grow together, complain together, and huddle together," I said. "And if I go a little far, you can tell me to jump out the window. And if I think you guys are going too far, maybe I will tell you to jump out the window. But the most important thing is that whoever jumps, one of us is always going to be outside waiting to break our fall. This network…"

Perry stood up and started walking towards the door.

"Perry? Where are you going?"

"To see my barber, Mike. I have a five o'clock hair appointment and I don't want to keep him waiting."

And with that, he was gone.

But Perry was like that. He had little time for my eccentricities and misbehavior. He was never rude. He just knew instinctively how far he could push it.

A couple of weeks later, during one of my regular trips to the West Coast, Perry said he was going down to a casting session.

"Hey, I've got nothing to do. I'll come with you."

"Oh no you don't," said Perry. "You'll upset everybody if you go down there. Let me go down, and I'll let you know what happened."

There was no use arguing, so I just sat in Perry's office with my feet on his desk.

"And you can take your feet off my desk too," he said.

I glared at Perry and leaned back a little further, rearranging my heels on his paperwork. So Perry strode over to the desk, picked up my feet and slid a piece of cardboard underneath them.

Perry died a few years ago, but just before he passed away I understand he told someone, "Don't tell Mike right away. He's got such a big mouth, he'll tell everybody."

Jack Schneider's presidency lasted about a year before he was promoted to president of the CBS Broadcast Group. His replacement, John Reynolds, a senior vice president from the West Coast, did not like me very much, and I heard rumors that he wanted to fire me.

Rather than being forced out by Reynolds, I thought I would force his hand. I marched into his office and offered my resignation. Reynolds looked stunned. As he tried to talk me out of it, I realized that he needed me far more than I needed him. His position depended upon the ratings even more than mine. And I was his best chance of winning. From that moment on I operated almost autonomously within his administration.

In fact, I am sure that was Paley's idea when he appointed him. Because although the chairman left the day-to-day running of the company in the hands of Dr. Frank Stanton, he maintained an almost obsessive interest in the program department. And he wanted me there as his right hand.

Paley called me daily, sometimes three times a day, from early morning to late at night. During weekends, if I was out with my wife shopping at Sears Roebuck or at the mall in White Plains, I was expected to call in from a pay phone. And if Paley was on one of his many extended stays at his home at Lyford Cay in the Bahamas he would call from there too. Paley wanted to know the overnight numbers and my thoughts on the previous evening's programming as well as the schedule for the week ahead. He wanted to know what interesting program ideas I had heard about, how our stars were doing and what the competition was up to. Sometimes, when I was on the West Coast, he would call in the early evening to discuss the latest episode of a show I had not yet seen because of the three-hour time difference.

Working for Paley could be frustrating. He never came out and said exactly what he wanted. Instead, his orders took the form of suggestions. When Paley said that we "might do this" or we "could do that" he meant that it would be done, or else. He was notorious for hedging his bets. In making a decision he might ask for my opinion and end the conversation by saying that he agreed. Then, later the same day, he would reverse course, saying that perhaps we ought to be more cautious. The following day he would revert to our initial idea. That way, if a program worked he could say he had been right all along. And if something went wrong he could claim we made the decision against his better judgment.

In 1961, I passed on a sitcom called *Car 54, Where Are You?*, a comedy about New York cops starring Joe E. Ross, one of the co-stars of *Sgt. Bilko*. Instead, I signed a sitcom about a TV comedy writer, called *The Dick Van Dyke Show*, written by and starring Carl Reiner. When the two shows opened the new season, *Car 54* on NBC at 8:30 p.m. on Sundays and *The Dick Van Dyke Show* on CBS at 8 p.m. on Tuesdays, Paley was livid. *Car 54* was a huge success while *Dick Van Dyke* was getting hammered.

Paley called me into his lavish, wood-paneled office, decorated with post-impressionist and cubist artworks that looked as though they belonged in the Museum of Modern Art. Seated behind his desk, dressed in a dark, tailored suit, he looked at me very seriously, and said: "Young man, why didn't you take *Car 54?* That's a big hit on NBC that we could have had on CBS."

"I know, Mr. Paley. But I thought *The Dick Van Dyke Show* was more CBS's quality and taste."

"There is no such thing as quality and taste with no audience."

I left Paley's office with my tail between my legs. I knew there was potential in *The Dick Van Dyke Show*, but there was no denying the numbers were bad. So the next season I took a gamble by keeping the program but moving it to a new time slot, Wednesdays at 9:30, following *The Beverly Hillbillies*. Sure enough, the numbers rose considerably and *The Dick Van Dyke Show* became an instant hit.

Paley was quick to congratulate himself on this excellent programming strategy.

"That's a good little show you've got there," Paley said the next time I saw him. "That's quality CBS. You know, you should have scheduled it on Wednesdays at nine-thirty p.m. in the first place."

"Yes, sir," I said. "And I am sure glad you objected to it at eight o'clock."

"Well, I was right, wasn't I?"

"You certainly were right, Mr. Paley. And boy, has it got legs too. It's going to stay."

"You bet it is," said Paley. "That's CBS quality programming and CBS quality comedy."

Car 54 disappeared off the air in a few seasons, while *The Dick Van Dyke Show* kept going for five years. And all thanks to Paley. He was the best second guesser in the world. His indecision caused no end of programming complications and last-minute panics. Weeks before the start of the 1964 season, he nearly gave us all a heart attack when he suddenly decided he did not like our new sitcom, *The Munsters*.

"You're not going to put that thing on the air?" Paley said. "It's a perfectly terrible show. It's not CBS."

I did not dare tell Paley this was the same show he had approved months earlier.

"Well, Mr. Paley, *The Munsters* is meant for children," I said, explaining that we had scheduled the program for 7:30 p.m. to catch the early evening family audience, much as *Disneyland* had done years earlier. "We think it could be a strong show."

"I think it's perfectly disgusting," said Paley. "It's an embarrassment to our network. Isn't there something you can do to fix it?"

After Paley hung up I called our West Coast producer.

"Are you kidding me?" he said. "That show starts in a few weeks. We can't drop it now, and we can't change it either."

There was nothing left to do but run the show. The season started and *The Munsters* was a smash. The next day at lunch Paley commended me on the show.

"You know, Mike, I am glad I told you to make those changes to *The Munsters*. Last night's show was a real improvement on the pilot and it had some wonderful qualities. The Munsters might be a little larger than life, but somehow they grow on you. We turned them into real people."

Of course, we had not changed a single thing.

Paley was liberal with his praise, but only when discussing his own decisions. He rarely, if ever, complimented anything or anyone else. So it could be difficult to tell whether your work was actually being appreciated. If I told Paley we had nine of the top 10 shows, Paley would say, "That damned NBC always hangs in for one." Once, when I told him that I had just concluded a meeting with Chagall, in which the artist had agreed to film a documentary about his life, Paley replied: "You couldn't get Matisse?"

I had always been an upbeat character. I was a salesman, and selling something required a positive attitude. Now, I was faced with a boss who was always nitpicking. When he promoted me to head of programming, Paley said, "Don't tell me what we are doing well. I can't help with that. Just tell me where we are failing." As a consequence, I learned never to say that anything was good.

I was at my most negative when we were setting the next season's schedule. I would open the meeting by telling Paley we had a rough year ahead with some very strong competition. Then I would introduce each evening's schedule and our new shows with the caveat that perhaps Paley was not going to like them. I became such an expert at putting programs down that Paley started calling me "Mr. Downbeat" or "Mr. Negative," and he would sometimes turn to the others in the room and say, "Pay no attention to him. He's the eternal pessimist."

Despite my anxieties I loved my new job. For the first time in my career I was dealing directly with the boss. I had total control. And although Paley never said or did much to let me know he approved of my work, I think he liked me because I won season after season..

I got to work immediately, straightening out the 1965-66 schedule and dealing with the day-to-day crises that running the most successful programming department throws at you. My days were a succession of meetings and lunches with agents, producers and stars. I became a fixture at Le Pavillon and La Côte Basque and I made very liberal use of my expense account, often to the finance department's horror.

On one occasion a finance officer came to see me at CBS with a very grave look on his face.

"Mike, your expense account is excessive. What is this? Twelve hundred dollars for lunch at '21?'"

"I was having lunch with Orson Welles, and he ate a lot, and he drank a lot of fine wine."

"But that's a terrible amount. How will that look on the books?"

"I'll make a deal with you. If you never come in to me again and talk about my expenses, this meeting is over. But if you do come in again, I promise you the next one will be double."

The guy never came back.

Apart from entertaining stars I would occasionally stop and have a drink with the boys after work. But most days I would head straight for Grand Central to catch the train home to Chappaqua for 8 p.m. or 9 p.m. I also tried to get out to the Coast at least twice a month; there was a lot of fun to be had out there.

Meanwhile, Aubrey had left CBS in a bad way, and I had to make some very important programming decisions straight away. My rejigging of the schedule in the winter of 1964-65 had pulled CBS slightly ahead of NBC in the ratings, but there would have to be a number of changes if we were to put any distance between ourselves and our rivals in the forthcoming season.

The industry itself was changing dramatically. Just a few years after Jim Aubrey had ridiculed color television to Paley, sales of color sets were outstripping black-and-white by three to one. Though the vast majority of homes still had black-and-white televisions, every one of the top 10 shows was broadcast in color.

Dumping Brasselle's *The Baileys of Balboa* and *The Cara Williams Show* was a no-brainer. But I also had to make some tough decisions, including whether to pull the plug on Herb Brodkin's shows *The Defenders*, *The Nurses*, and a new series that had not yet aired, called *Coronet Blue*. The first two shows were suffering, and I had grave concerns about the so far untested *Coronet Blue*. Even though I had a great deal of respect for Brodkin, especially after his success with *The Defenders*, the numbers suggested that his realistic style was falling out of favor with the television audience.

There was going to be no easy way to break the news to Brodkin. He was a very tough man, tall, thin, light-haired, and prone to bouts of extreme anger. I do not think he ever made an appointment to see me. He would just storm into my office, with his agent Ted Ashley in tow, and bawl me out. Ted may have been my friend, but Herb was his meal ticket, so there was very little he could do to calm Brodkin down. When I told him I was canceling his show, he took it about as well as could be expected. He stormed out of my office and refused to speak to me for the next two years. High drama became a facet of everyday life at CBS.

When I was not juggling crises with stars and producers I would usually be sucked into corporate dilemmas. I do not think I had been in the job more than a few months before Gordon Manning called from our news department at 10 o'clock one morning. A group of civil rights demonstrators had embarked on a march from Selma to Montgomery, Alabama, and Gordon wanted to interrupt daytime programming to cover it. I told him he could have an hour and I pulled whichever show was scheduled for that time slot.

Within a few minutes the lights on my telephone console started blinking. Southern affiliate station owners wanted to know why we were cutting into their air time. The sales department wanted to know why we were wasting valuable advertising minutes. I reassured them that it was only temporary. But looking at my television screen, as the number of demonstrators grew, it became clear that we were witnessing a momentous occasion.

Manning called again. "They're still marching, Mike. And the crowds are getting bigger. Can we stay with it?"

"Stay with it."

"I've got to stay with it."

"Stay with it."

At lunchtime, the vice president in charge of sales strode into my office to ask why the march was still being broadcast.

"You're killing us, Mike. You've got to stop that coverage for a while. Everyone will get it on the evening news, anyway."

"But this is happening now," I said. "I'll talk to Gordon, but if this thing keeps getting bigger, we're going to have to stick with it."

As I expected, Manning insisted that we keep broadcasting and I agreed. As the afternoon wore on, the telephone calls from southern affiliates became angrier. I even heard from a few southern senators and a governor too. CBS president Frank Stanton must have been getting similar calls because in the early afternoon he called me.

"Mike, I talked to the news department and they feel they have to stay with this. What is your feeling?"

"Well, Frank, I think we have to stay with it too. It's a major news event. We'd be crazy not to cover it."

Stanton said, "Very good." And hung up.

We must have canceled the whole day's programming. A lot of people gave me hell for it. We were branded as left wing. But a great change was taking place in American society. Just a year earlier riots had broken out in Harlem, and a few months after the Selma to Montgomery march, the Watts neighborhood in L.A. would go the same way. It seemed only natural for television to cover such an event. People accused us of fanning the flames. But as far as we were concerned these things were happening. We covered them exactly the same as a newspaper would. The only difference was that television was so much more powerful than an article or a photograph.

Although we took quite a beating for broadcasting the Selma march, morale at CBS was high during 1965. With Aubrey gone it was as though the network had a new lease on life—a fact that was symbolized when we moved offices from 485 Madison Avenue to West 52nd Street and Sixth Avenue. It was a move of only two long blocks, but entering the new building—quickly nicknamed "Black Rock" because of its dark exterior—was like entering a different world.

Black Rock was more than five years in the making, from when Paley bought the land in the late 1950s to when we eventually moved in. In many respects it was Frank Stanton's building. It was he who championed the move and who chose Saarinen, the architect. The entire structure mirrored Stanton's meticulous attention to detail. The sleek, black granite exterior, rising almost 500 feet devoid of setbacks and frills, was both imposing and austere. The building was dignified, elegant, refined, and clinical, with almost 2,000 gray, heat-absorbing windows staring blankly out onto the street.

Inside, Stanton had employed his friend, the designer Florence Knoll, to oversee every floor and office, from the dark gray carpets and Formica desks to the low-slung, artificial leather couches and chrome-legged chairs. Even the plants and flower arrangements were regimented. I remember Stanton doing a walk-through of the 34th floor and being aghast to see that the tiles were the wrong shade of white. He had them all replaced.

We were forbidden from adding a personal touch to our offices in any way. Every painting, print and photograph that appeared on a wall at Black Rock had to be approved by the CBS Art Committee. Indeed, the only room that escaped Stanton's regimentation was Paley's, which, as at 485 Madison, was decorated with mahogany furniture, early 20th-century artworks and a dark green carpet.

Paley insisted on having a restaurant on the ground floor. He told me he wanted it to be somewhere where the secretaries could have a nice lunch for $5, though how he expected secretaries to be able to afford such a lunch I will never know. Either way, true to form, Paley changed his mind multiple times about the restaurant, and we must have had three or four businesses in there before Paley finally settled on one.

I was given an enormous corner office, number 3438, on the 34th floor. It offered a breathtaking panorama of Manhattan and a bird's-eye view of the Henry Moore sculpture in the courtyard of the Museum of Modern Art. I went out and bought a good pair of binoculars the first chance I got.

Yet I found the sterility of the room suffocating. So, a couple of weeks after moving in I brought a picture of my family into the office and picked up the phone to the building maintenance department.

"That goddamn picture you hung on my wall has fallen down. Could you get somebody up here to do something about it."

Within a few minutes someone was standing in my doorway with a hammer and nails.

"Here," I said, handing him the picture frame and pointing towards a bare spot on the wall. "I don't know how it came down, but I think it was supposed to go there."

Once the picture was up I could relax. The desk and carpet would have to go too, but I could wait for those. The portrait of my family was a start. And I had a lot of work to do.

14.

Prime Time, Baby!

"He was the most canny politician when it came to how to work the system. He also was the wittiest, funniest, most charming guy you would ever want to work with, terribly funny and so bright."
– Interview with Jerry Leider about Mike Dann, June 2008.

If you run into trouble in the theater business you can always close a theater or a movie house for a week or two. If you run into a problem in the publishing industry you may decide to print only a handful of books one year. But in television, you can never go dark. Every week, 49 half hours of prime time must be filled with the most attractive, engaging, addictive programming, not to mention 12-and-a-half hours of morning and daytime shows too. Your role as a network executive plays out live, 24 hours a day, seven days a week under the most extraordinary of circumstances: the death of a President, civil unrest, a country at war. Prime time is the essence—the life force—of the network. Without it the company loses its character. Advertisers have nothing to sell against, viewers have nothing to identify with, and producers, actors and directors have nothing to aim for.

I did not make prime time. I merely contributed to it, both as an assistant to Pat Weaver during the early years of television and as a network executive during CBS's unbroken 14-year run. But if I can make one claim to television immortality it is that more than any one of my peers, I made prime time work. I programmed and counter-programmed. I turned mediocre shows into hits by moving them out of one time slot and into another. Between 1958 and 1965 I helped first Lou Cowan and then Jim Aubrey keep CBS at the top of the ratings. From 1965 onwards, although there would always be a presidential figurehead above me, I steered CBS from ratings victory to ratings victory. And as I pulled CBS higher and higher each season, I gave myself even further to fall. My biggest fear throughout the mid- to late 1960s, over and above my natural revulsion at the thought of losing, was that CBS would slip from the number-one spot while I was in charge. Not on my watch.

History may have judged Jim Aubrey to have turned CBS into the Hillbilly Network. But I was just as guilty of chasing the numbers . Once I was in complete control, I could have weeded out the low-quality sitcoms and westerns and shifted our focus towards prestigious, thoughtful programming. Instead, I ditched Herb Brodkin's shows and kept *The Beverly Hillbillies*, *Petticoat Junction*, and *Gomer Pyle*. During the 1960s, the decade when I was at the height of my network powers, broadcast television never achieved even a fraction of the potential dreamed of by Pat Weaver and Edward Murrow. Instead, it embraced the vast wasteland derided by Newton Minow. It was driven there by the ever tightening race between the three networks. And no one, and I mean no one, was more skilled at playing by the numbers than I.

Scheduling is the greatest crap shoot in the history of entertainment and possibly the single greatest challenge a program man faces. You have to balance the merits of a single show with the programs that precede and follow it, and the alternative being offered by the competition. On top of that you are dealing with the ficklest of customers, the television viewer, who is stuck fast in his or her viewing habits.

I learned early on that where I scheduled a show was often far more important than the actual content, an idea which ran contrary to everything that Pat believed. When *Hawaii Five-O* debuted on CBS at 8 o'clock on Thursdays it won just 22 percent of the audience and barely registered in the top 100 television programs on television. *Hawaii Five-O* was a well conceived, well executed and visually attractive show. But it was competing with two strong dramas on NBC, *Daniel Boone* from 7:30 p.m. to 8:30 p.m. and *Ironsides* from 8:30 p.m. to 9:30 p.m. So just before Christmas I called Jack Lord, who played Steve McGarrett, and told him I was switching the show to Wednesdays at 10 o'clock.

"The ratings are down?" Lord said.

"You bet. I'm moving you up against a repeat of *The Outsider*."

"But that's a top ten show."

"Yeah, but you're facing a bigger problem right now. Besides, you've got a good show. You'll have a lead in off *Medical Center*, and *The Outsider* is looking tired. You'll be a smash."

Sure enough, *Hawaii Five-O* rocketed up the ratings into the top 10, and *The Outsider* was canceled the following year.

When it came to scheduling new shows, I quickly learned audiences would only "discover" a new sitcom if it followed a hit comedy or, even better, was hammocked between two established programs. That was why *Dick Van Dyke* flopped on Tuesdays, between *Marshall Dillon* and *The Many Loves of Dobie Gillis*, but did tremendously well coming straight after *The Beverly Hillbillies*.

Even following my own rules and trusting my instincts guaranteed only partial success. In 1966, I had what I thought was a sensational sitcom called *Run Buddy Run*, starring jazz trumpeter Jack Sheldon. I hammocked it between *Gilligan's Island* and *The Lucy Show* at 8 o'clock on Mondays. But the audience never came, and I had to pull it after less than six months. Likewise, in 1967 I found what I thought was the most successful comedy of my career, a sitcom starring Paula Prentiss and her husband Dick Benjamin called *He and She*. After I scheduled the show for 9:30 on Wednesdays following *The Beverly Hillbillies* and *Green Acres* I was sure I had a hit on my hands. But despite winning an Emmy for comedy writing, *He and She* was canceled after only one season because the numbers were so low.

Losing quality shows like *He and She* and *Run Buddy Run* was always a major disappointment. But when you have brought a program that far and scheduled it right, and it still flops, you have to admit to yourself that there was nothing more you could do. Besides, there were enough hits in between to make the entire process worthwhile. And some of those shows, even the sitcoms, raised the standards a little bit higher than the Hillbillies.

Perry Lafferty was central to this achievement. His eye for quality and mass appeal rarely failed. And I seldom resisted his ideas. However, I was a little worried when, in the mid-1960s, he handed me the script for a sitcom about a group of Allied soldiers in a prisoner of war camp.

"Perry, are you nuts? A comedy about the Nazis?"

"Just read the script, Mike. It's very funny."

"America isn't ready."

"Just read the script."

As a rule, I never read scripts. And as I flicked through the pages pretending to digest the program, Perry handed me a photograph of the main Nazi protagonists, Colonel Wilhelm Klink and Sergeant Hans Schultz. Klink, a thin guy with glasses, was played by Werner Klemperer, the son of the famed composer Otto Klemperer. His sidekick, Sergeant Schultz, was a tubby guy played by John Banner. The two of them looked so funny together in their Nazi get up.

"As long as we make the Nazis out to be the biggest idiots on earth," Perry reassured me, "we'll be fine."

The more I thought about it the more I laughed. Here was a really funny show that just 20 years after the war could bring Nazis to prime time as figures of fun.

Hogan's Heroes was a gang comedy. The leader, Bob Crane, was not a comic like some of his supporting actors, but he was a wonderful actor and he had a lovely flavor to him. Off camera he could be a bit of an odd fellow—he was murdered under mysterious circumstances in 1978—but he was a nice guy to work with. Crane was supported by a wonderful cast of different races and nationalities. There was the Englishman Richard Dawson, who played Corporal Newkirk, and the African-American Ivan Dixon, who played staff sergeant "Kinch" Kinchloe. And if I was ever in any doubt about the way *Hogan* might be received by American Jews it was tempered by the inclusion of Robert Clary as Corporal Louis LeBeau. Clary was a French-born Jew and Holocaust survivor who had spent his teenage years at the Buchenwald concentration camp. If he thought the show was worthwhile, then that was good enough for me.

Hogan's Heroes was one of the few sets that Perry would allow me to visit and I loved to drop by, joke around with the cast and watch shooting and rehearsals. The show was my idea of television at its best—well written, well acted and always carrying with it that sense that it was dealing with issues bigger than just itself, as *M*A*S*H* would do a few years later. I slotted the program in at 8:30 on Friday night after the adventure comedy show *The Wild, Wild West* and before *Gomer Pyle*, which was quite a lineup for our rivals to contend with.

Other successes were more down to luck than anything else. In 1966, we were contractually obliged to take a couple of half-hour shows from Desilu Studios as part of our deal to bring Lucy back to television. But their offerings for that year were dire, the only bright spot being a pilot for a half-hour show called *Mission: Impossible*. Since we had an hour-long gap to fill on Saturday nights at 9 o'clock, where we were being outgunned by *The Lawrence Welk Show* on ABC and *Saturday Night at the Movies* on NBC, I suggested to Desilu that if they could turn *Mission: Impossible* into an hour-long show, everyone would be happy. *Mission: Impossible* may not have dealt with social issues like a Herb Brodkin show, but it was a fabulous action-drama, probably one of the best of its genre, and proved stiff competition for our rivals.

Searching for new shows was a year-round vocation. As pilots like *Hogan's Heroes* and *Mission: Impossible* came across my desk I always had in mind where they could possibly fit into the next season's schedule. Each winter the process became an all-consuming obsession as we looked ahead to the following fall. The busiest two months of the year were January and February, when I would build my schedule and then announce the coming lineup. Because CBS was the market leader, we always announced our schedule first. I chose Washington's birthday as a fitting date. It was conspicuous, it reinforced our image as the market leader and my sales department could then go out and sell my schedule quicker than anybody else's. Besides, I always had the option of making last-minute changes in the spring.

From January 1, I had about seven weeks to finalize the upcoming schedule. I would begin by taking out an enormous, white, magnetic board that I had designed after years of struggling with paper. The board was about 3 feet tall and at least 6 feet wide. Down the left-hand side in black lettering were the days of the week beginning with our most important day, Sunday. Along the top of the board, in bold black numbers, were the seven half-hour, prime-time slots from 7:30 p.m. to 10:30 p.m. Within each day, there were three blank slots, one for CBS, one for ABC, and one for NBC. The first thing I would do before giving the schedule serious consideration was to populate the CBS slots with red magnetic cards showing the current schedule, leaving out any shows I thought were unworthy of inclusion the following season. Next, I would populate the ABC slots with tan-colored magnetic cards and the NBC slots with blue magnetic cards, bearing some resemblance to our competitors' current schedules and any intelligence I had gathered on what they might be planning for the next season. Stepping back from the board I would cast my eye along the red CBS row, analyzing our program order, and then cast my eye down through the time slots—red, tan, blue, red, tan, blue—to see the competition we were up against.

All of this took place in a conference room with a couple of dozen trusted colleagues from the research, sales and programming departments. By the time I stepped back from the board there would be about a half-dozen empty slots and I would say, to nobody in particular, "Okay guys, what are we going to do?"

Then the fun would begin. Off to the side was another magnetic board—the development board—which held our new hour and half-hour shows, which would have to be incorporated into the schedule. I had so many strong shows that I replaced as few as possible, but there was always going to be a small number of changes. We might place a new drama series into a time slot when our competitors were running kids' shows or we might pit a variety show against a couple of westerns. I would also be sure to hammock a new sitcom between, or at the very least have it follow, established hits. Lagging shows that I still believed to have some potential were moved into different time positions, and those that I no longer had confidence in were tossed on a table nearby.

The scheduling board was like an enormous, multi-colored puzzle, a game of strategy where I had to make all of my moves without knowing for sure what my opponent was going to do. That was the penalty I paid for programming the leading network and making my calls before anyone else.

When I scheduled a new show, it gave me equal parts pleasure and concern. Every one had beaten incredible odds just to make it this far. Of the thousands of ideas pitched over lunches, dinners and business meetings, they had made it to the 100 or so scripts that were seriously considered. We made only about 25 pilots a year, and only about a half dozen of those pilots made it onto the scheduling board. Of these shows only two or three would survive into a second season. It was a wonder anyone made a living in the industry at all.

Of course, shows were not just added to the schedule on my gut instinct and the say-so of a couple of my staff. When Frank Stanton had joined CBS 20 years earlier he had personally pioneered a "program analyzer'" that the network could use to determine the reaction of focus groups to new shows. Usually, we would take a studio audience or a random selection of people off the street and sit them down in front of a pilot with a little box that had two colored buttons. As we screened the pilot, the audience would be invited to press the green button if they saw something they liked and the red button if they saw something they did not like. After the screening they would be asked to fill out a short questionnaire and to rate the show.

I was never entirely convinced that the program analyzer delivered a useful result. The only data I trusted were the numbers from our research department the night after the show aired. I could show the same program to two audiences, and one might like it and the other might not. Sometimes there is just a mood in a room. It is very hard to measure such things. Only after coming back over a few weeks can an audience really know whether it likes what it is seeing. I never believed in the test. But it was a good way of hedging decision making. After all, if the focus group tested well, what more evidence did I need that I had made a sound programming decision in buying a particular show?

Needless to say, with one eye fixed on the Nielsens and the other trying to watch our competition, focus groups and budgets, the schedule never reflected my personal tastes. Occasionally, I kept a show because it was so good, its middling rating could be overlooked. But more often than not, the highest numbers determined which were our funniest, most exciting shows.

If all our shows had been up to the standard of, say, Herbert Brodkin's, then the process of screening the pilots would have been bearable. But the reality was that many of our shows were terrible. Though I could get away with never reading scripts and I could avoid programs once they were on the schedule, there was no way I could escape the screening process.

It was company policy for screenings to take place at 11 a.m. and 4 p.m., the optimal times for creativity and judgment according to some company schmuck. My viewing room was just across from my office, furnished with very comfortable chairs in front of a beautiful, big screen. Viewings were always conducted in silence and only ever one show at a time. Sometimes, I got so bored that I excused myself, saying I had to go to the bathroom and that they should keep running the film without me. Then, I would go back to my office and get some work done, returning for the very end.

Sometimes Paley would join me for the viewings. He could get quite restless on these occasions, and I always made sure to order food from one of his favorite restaurants, the Stage Deli. When the food arrived—hot sourdough bread; beautiful sandwiches, thick with mustard and piled high with corned beef, tongue and pastrami; pickles and coffee—I would see Paley wrinkle his nose and look towards the table.

"Where'd you get those sandwiches from, Mike?"

"From your friend Max Osnas at the Stage Deli, Mr. Paley."

Paley's face would light up and he would keep glancing towards the sandwiches every minute or so.

"You want me to stop the film, Mr. Paley?"

"Oh no, no, don't stop. Just leave the lights on."

Then Paley would reach over for the food and make his way through two or three enormous sandwiches. When the show was over his first comment would be about the high standard of the sandwiches, particularly the tongue, which he liked as long as it was only the tip and very lean.

As with all of his decision-making, Paley could change his mind about a pilot multiple times. First he liked it, then he hated it, then he liked it again. So I learned always to take his multiple reactions as the temporary opinions of an ongoing trial.

Indeed my biggest problem was not so much working out how to plan the schedule, but how to get the schedule past Paley. When the time came for the scheduling presentation, he would call in the sales department, the research department and the programming department and quiz them on my suggestions.

After our move to Black Rock, scheduling meetings were always held in a windowless 34th-floor conference room. I would stand at the front, next to the scheduling board, with my outline for the season already drawn up and the new shows sitting expectantly on the development board off to the side. In the middle of the room was a circular table, where Paley, Stanton and a couple of senior executives such as the presidents of the CBS Broadcast Group and CBS-TV would be seated, along with the research director, Jay Eliasberg.

I would begin by outlining the schedule, highlighting our strengths and weaknesses, ever mindful of not appearing too positive in front of Paley. Then I would turn to the crucial few hours of programming that would inevitably need to be filled by new shows. For the next hour or so, Paley, Stanton and the others would call out ideas while I shuffled the cards on the board like a game show assistant. My strategy was to try to keep as close to my original plan as possible without seeming to force the schedule down Paley's throat.

While I was working for Henry Jaffe, during the months between NBC and CBS, he taught me never to go into a meeting with two or more people where I did not already know the outcome. So whenever I had to make a presentation I would always talk with the major players beforehand. Sometimes I would make concessions. Other times I would kick a few people up the ass. But I always knew before I stepped into that conference room that I had enough people on my side to get the schedule through. The sales department, the research department, the engineering department and the affiliate relations chief would be all lined up. I would make my presentation and then the boss would go around the table asking the advice of each of the department heads. One guy would say, "I think Mike is right." The next would say, "I think it's a good point." And the guy next to him would say, "Well, I was a little worried at first, but I think I have figured out a way around any problems we might have."

Paley knew the pilots well, and he loved arguing and discussing programming strategy. He would ask why I took out a particular show or why I chose to replace it with something he was not too keen on, then turn to Perry or Eliasberg and ask for their opinion, which almost always matched my own. Sure, a number of decisions went over my head. But I managed to keep the bulk of my picks intact. Meanwhile, to keep Paley happy, I always ordered an enormous lunch from the Stage Deli.

The finest line to walk was convincing Paley I had made the right choices without seeming too positive. When *Mission: Impossible* looked to be a hit after its first week, Paley asked if I thought we could replicate the success every week.

"Mr. Paley, we made the first one," I said. "The producer says he can make more. And I have to go with what the producer is telling me. That's the best I can give you."

To which Paley would smile.

Once the schedule was agreed it was time to sell it to the affiliates. Every year, usually around May, CBS would hold a convention, where I would give a presentation about the upcoming season. I always liked to start the process by giving them a bit of a performance.

"Now, there's three things you want," I would say.

"You guys in the South, who don't like Fred Friendly, you want us to be more conservative… No chance!"

And I would get a big laugh.

"You guys," I would say, pointing at a section of the audience, "want more commercial time for local sales…. No way!"

Another big laugh.

"And you are all complaining that we interrupt the shows too often with specials… If you keep complaining, I'm going to put on more!"

And the room would erupt. These important guys could not get enough of being told to go to hell.

"You know what I'm going to do? I've got a show here that's too good for you. It's so good I'm only going to show it in my house."

I loved to perform. And as I turned to the fall lineup, explaining our decisions and introducing new shows, I would keep the jokes rolling. There would be howls of laughter and applause. I never said, "Now you're going to see a great show" or something like that. It would always be, "You think this one is bad? Wait until the next one. It's worse!" The convention was probably the highlight of my year.

After that it was down to the mundane business of keeping the schedule ticking, which was no mean feat with so many casts and crews working concurrently. In the movie business people are usually signed for a single project. But in television the relationship is a lot more complicated. The schedule is a lifeline for hundreds of families and careers. It can continue for years, as it did with Lucy and the cast of *The Beverly Hillbillies*, or it can last for a season, or even less. When I canceled a show, I effectively sacked over a dozen people, including producers, writers, directors, agents and actors. To a lot of people I was a shitheel and, to be honest, in some cases they were right. But just imagine turning around to anyone you have had a business relationship with for one, two, five or ten years, people you admire and are fond of, and saying: "The show's canceled." Those same people screamed and hollered, they threatened and cajoled, they wrote letters and tried to outflank me, but at the end of the day the numbers spoke for themselves.

Which was not to say that I was totally a slave to the ratings. In the mid- to late 1960s I succeeded in getting a number of quality shows on television. Under Schneider, Reynolds and later his replacement, Tom Dawson, I had full control to make any decision I wanted.

My first big hit came about after an uncomfortable meeting with David Susskind. David had been in one of his usual bellicose moods, ranting about ideas he felt were not being properly considered by CBS. One suggestion was for a TV version of Arthur Miller's *Death of a Salesman*. And following the meeting, as I walked down the street, I thought to myself that this idea might just work. Later that day, I put in a couple of telephone calls and arranged for a meeting with Arthur in my office.

After greeting Arthur and asking him to sit down, I cut straight to the point, that David had suggested a television version of *Death of a Salesman* and that although I had my doubts about how it would translate onto the small screen, I was willing to give it a shot.

"Mike, I think it'd be a good television play," Arthur said. And then his eyes lit up. "You know, if we could get Millie Dunnock and Lee J. Cobb to do it, it might be even better than the original performance."

Dunnock and Cobb had appeared in the stage production of *Death of a Salesman* in the late 1940s. And Arthur explained that at that time both actors had actually been a little too young for their parts. He said that he had always envisaged Willy Loman being played by someone closer to his 60s than his 40s, and that Cobb would now be perfect.

Finding sponsors for such a show was never going to be easy. Advertisers still shied away from big-budget spectaculars. But Paley agreed that in this case the network would pay for the production. The cost, nearly $500,000, was only marginally offset by our success in persuading Xerox to sponsor the airtime.

Meanwhile, Arthur and David were busy hustling Dunnock and Cobb to appear in the show. Arthur even agreed to make some minor adjustments to the script for television. David also brought in a young Gene Wilder to play one of Willy's sons and the director Alex Segal to pull the whole thing together.

Now Lee J. Cobb was not the easiest man to deal with, and Alex Segal was a temperamental director. The two hit it off badly. Segal was used to giving orders to lesser actors than Dunnock and Cobb. Meanwhile, Cobb did not like anyone telling him what to do. Over the next four weeks, as they rehearsed in a big lot next to Television City, Perry informed me of a deteriorating relationship between the two men. I had to fly out to the Coast on more than one occasion to mediate after fights between Segal and Cobb. But they got the job done. *Death of a Salesman* was filmed over four days. And the result, when it was aired in May 1966, was breathtaking. Even Jack Gould was bowled over. His review, which I still cherish today, began:

"An evening of exalted theater came to television last night in a revelation of Arthur Miller's "Death of a Salesman" that will stand as the supreme understanding of the tragedy of Willy Loman.

"For television the play is a veritable landmark in studio drama, an occasion of power so shattering and poignancy so delicate that there is no earlier parallel to cite. Lee J. Cobb's portrayal of Willy was richer and deeper than it was on the stage. But it was the stoic beauty and pathos of Mildred Dunnock's performance as the salesman's wife that achieved an enlarged and unforgettable nobility on the home screen. It will remain forever a cherished treasure of the acting art."

Quite simply, the production was a triumph for television, which Gould went on to say had bettered the stage version by adding "its own incisiveness, sensitivity and perspective to Mr. Miller's drama, personalizing the agony of failure with an intensity and intimacy not possible in a theater where there is no close-up. A modern classic was not merely rendered; it was improved upon by a branch of theatrical expression utilizing its own creative resources."

After years of toiling at the Hillbilly Network, I finally had something of which I knew even Pat would have been proud. And I went on to repeat that success at every opportunity.

I always believed that television was particularly effective for one-man performances. In 1966, I scheduled John Gielgud's *Ages of Man*, produced by David Susskind. And the following year, I signed Hal Holbrook's *Mark Twain Tonight!* Many advertisers were reticent to support the show because Twain was a liberal, and we had a lot of difficulties getting it on the air. Hal was a close friend of mine, and he thanked me regularly in years to come for putting him on the air as Mark Twain. Hal imitated Twain to a tee. He would stand in the wings, and suddenly you would see this puff of cigar smoke as he walked out on stage to huge applause. He would take out his watch, lay it carefully on the side and then launch into a monologue that was simply spellbinding.

I also relied heavily on my good friend Sol Hurok. After I assumed control, *S. Hurok Presents* became an annual fixture on CBS. Not one of the shows turned a profit, but they elevated the prestige of the network no end. In 1966, we showcased more stars in one evening than Aubrey had managed during his entire CBS career: Marian Anderson, Van Cliburn, Isaac Stern, Andrés Segovia, the Bolshoi Ballet with Maya Plisetskaya, and the Ballets de Madrid. In years to follow we would add other stars such as the pianist Artur Rubinstein and the violinist David Oistrakh.

Working with such talent was unlike anything else I had experienced before. They had to be handled with kid gloves, in a very gentle and refined manner. Sol and I resumed our regular lunches at Le Pavillon and La Caravelle. He brought me into the center of New York's cultural life, and we had such good times. Of course, he had to keep reminding me how to order like a gentleman and how to conduct business at lunches, just as he had done during the 1950s. He was the man of the arts in the city at the time. I remember over one particular lunch Sol was very upset over plans to tear down the old Metropolitan Opera House because the opera company was relocating to the new Lincoln Center.

"You should keep both buildings," he said angrily in a heavy Yiddish accent, as though the decision had been mine. "Where am I supposed to put my audiences? Carnegie Hall just doesn't take enough people. Why are they knocking down a perfectly good building? They should keep both. I could fill them all!"

Sol could get almost any performer. But in 1968, the New York Times music critic Howard Taubman called me with a very interesting proposition. Taubman said that he knew the famously reclusive pianist Vladimir Horowitz and that he believed Horowitz might be persuaded to perform on television. I told Taubman that we would be delighted to accommodate Horowitz in any way possible and to convey to him our great interest in having him appear on our network. Finally, Taubman came back with an answer. Horowitz would perform. But he had a number of conditions, which included that he must be given ample time to rehearse, that everybody working around him wore rubber-soled shoes so that they did not make any distracting noise, and that the performance take place in Carnegie Hall.

"Done!" I said.

Naturally, everybody wanted to see Horowitz perform, so we allowed Taubman to draw up a list of those who would be invited. The performance was to be filmed and then broadcast later. I did not attend the event, but the following day I got a call saying Horowitz wanted to run through the whole thing again. Apparently, he had listened to the recording and picked up on certain things he did not like. So a second concert was held, and Horowitz oversaw the editing of the two versions to create what was, to his ear, a superior performance.

A few days before the broadcast, which had been scheduled for 9 o'clock on Sunday evening opposite *Bonanza*, I got a call from Taubman saying that Horowitz wanted to watch the show with me and then to go for dinner afterwards. I was not going to argue with such a request, so I arranged for a few members of staff and a waiter to be on hand at Black Rock that Sunday night. About a half hour before the performance, Taubman arrived with his wife. Soon afterwards Horowitz walked in with his wife, Wanda, the daughter of the great Toscanini, and his housekeeper. Horowitz and his wife were an odd-looking couple. Horowitz was a beanpole of a man, tall, gangly and balding, with dark eyes and a gaunt face. He looked as though he had just walked out of a casting session for *The Munsters*. Meanwhile, his wife Wanda was heavyset, like a giant washerwoman, with an ample bosom and a big tushie.

There were a couple of couches in my office and Horowitz sat down next to me. At 9 o'clock, as the titles came up, he turned sideways and lay back, putting his head in my lap and stretching his long legs out over the sofa.

Horowitz has got his head in my lap, I thought. *Dear God, what am I supposed to do?*

Horowitz's face was staring straight up towards mine. All I could do was look at the ceiling.

After a brief pause the pre-recorded Horowitz appeared on the television screen to a round of applause. He walked across the stage to his piano, sat down on the stool, raised his enormous hands to the keys, and began to play. Almost simultaneously the real life Horowitz, who had made himself at home in my crotch, raised his long fingers in the air, just in front of my face, and started to play along to the music.

While both Horowitzes played and played, I sat stone-cold still.

It was impossible to enjoy the performance. I could feel the sweat gathering on my brow. At one point, the real life Horowitz paused and grabbed my arm. "Wait. Wait. Wait," he said. "The horses are coming." And then he started playing again, his fingers beating out the notes in the air in front of my nose.

The entire concert proceeded in the same way. It only lasted an hour but it seemed like an eternity. When the final note was played, Horowitz lifted himself up and said, "What did you think?"

"An unforgettable evening," I said.

Following the performance we went for dinner at a nearby restaurant and I saw Horowitz to his car. Just as he was about to step in, he turned and said, "When do you get the numbers?"

"The numbers, Vladimir?"

"The ratings. When do you get the ratings for the show?"

Vladimir Horowitz is asking for his overnight ratings? I told him I would have them in the morning, and we agreed that he would call me when he was ready.

When the numbers came in they were terrible. It was unsurprising considering our competitors that night were the season premiere of *Bonanza*, on NBC, and *Zorba the Greek* on ABC. Later that day I heard the telephone ring and my secretary, Madeline, hurried in. "Mr. Horowitz is on the phone."

I picked up. "Vladimir," I said. "Vladimir, how are you?"

"Hello, Michael. Did you get the numbers?"

"Yes, and I can tell you that the audience last night was greater than all the performances you've played around the world all of your life."

There was a silence on the other end of the phone

"I don't believe you."

"It's true," I said. "Over four million homes, that's more than ten million viewers."

There was no need for Horowitz to know he had come a dismal third. After all, I was telling the truth. Even though he had scored a low rating, it far outstripped anything he achieved playing live venues. Horowitz was delighted. And though I never heard from him again, I like to think that the concert was one of the highlights of his career.

The question for me, though, at the start of the 1966 season, was how long I could keep getting pummeled by the number-one show in television, NBC's *Bonanza*.

15.

All the President's Men

It is hard to believe that *Bonanza*, a simple western about a father and his three sons, could dominate the ratings for almost a decade. Perhaps part of the appeal of the show was that at a time when our country was riven by conflict over civil rights and Vietnam, a swath of the American public found comfort in the Cartwright family, who solved each week's problems largely through talking to each other and by sticking to traditional Christian values. Of course, I did not care what attracted the audience to *Bonanza*. My problem was how to pry them away.

We pitted a variety of formats and more than a half dozen programs against the show: *General Electric Theater*, *The Jack Benny Program*, *The Real McCoys*, *General Electric True*, *The Judy Garland Show*, *My Living Doll*, *The Joey Bishop Show*, and *Perry Mason*. Every one of them failed. By 1966, *Bonanza* was celebrating its status as the top show on television for the third year in a row, and I was beginning to doubt we would ever find something to beat it.

It was while I was casting around for a Sunday night hit that I heard from my old friend Pat Weaver. Ten years after we had parted ways, and despite a number of setbacks, Pat was still heavily involved in the television industry. After his Pay TV venture failed, he had continued work as a consultant. And in 1966, he brought me an idea to resurrect the old *Garry Moore Show*. I thought a talk-variety show might be the perfect alternative to a western, so I scheduled it opposite *Bonanza* at 9 o'clock.

Unfortunately for Pat, *Bonanza* once again proved a clear hit in the ratings. After a few miserable months, Paley called and told me that he wanted Garry Moore off the air and that he expected to see a better replacement immediately. I felt awful for Pat, but there was nothing I could do. Besides, I was petrified. During the late 1960s, the ratings race was getting tighter and my reputation as a winner was at stake. There simply was not enough time to bring in a filmed show, so I was stuck with a live format.

I called a longtime agent friend, Sol Leon.

"Sol, I need a show for nine o'clock Sunday night."

"How about *The Smothers Brothers Comedy Hour*?"

"What do they do?"

Sol started to describe the show but I cut him short. "Look, just tell me when they can be ready."

"When do you need them by?"

"Well, it's January now, how about February fifth?"

The Smothers Brothers Comedy Hour was a comedy-variety show emceed by Dick and Tom Smothers. The brothers were clean-cut, all-American boys, dressed very properly in neat, unassuming suits. Dick played the role of the calmer, wiser brother, while Tom played the dumber, attention-seeking sibling, who frequently complained that "Mom always liked you best." As well as singing and performing as a duo, they appeared each week in various comedy sketches and musical routines with a cast of very talented writer-performers. Interspersing these performances was a phenomenal list of guest stars: Jefferson Airplane and George Burns, The Who and Mickey Rooney, The Doors and Jack Benny, Joan Baez and Sid Caesar, Ray Charles and Carol Burnett.

When I scheduled *The Smothers Brothers Comedy Hour*, and even after I attended rehearsals in Hollywood, I had no idea it would be such a success. I was delighted to sign the boys simply because I had nothing else and I could not go dark at 9 o'clock. Yet the show probably represented my greatest single programming decision. Not only did it go on to beat *Bonanza*—not every week, but some weeks—it also won more critical acclaim for me and my programming strategies than any series that I put on the air. It caught on instantly, especially among teens and 20-somethings, largely via word of mouth passed along in schools and colleges, burger joints and diners. Best of all for CBS, it attracted exactly the demographic our advertisers wanted to reach. Everyone congratulated me. Except Paley, of course, who just said, "You see? Didn't I tell you to get rid of Garry Moore?"

My joy, though, was short lived. The late 1960s was an extraordinary time in America. Not only were we fighting an unpopular war in Vietnam, but a social and cultural war was being fought on the campuses and in the streets and ghettoes of America. In their guest introductions and sketches, Dick and Tom riffed on issues of race and gender, war and peace. They quickly became an affront to southern affiliates, the bane of the White House and a constant pain in the ass for the CBS censors. But to their young, and growing, audience they were stars. Within a couple of months we had a top-20 hit on our hands, and I was negotiating a second season. But their sketches and asides only grew more contentious.

CBS had a defensive strategy. As with most shows, each *Smothers Brothers* script had to be vetted by program practices—the censors—before the show went on the air. We had a censor on the West Coast, Charlie Pettijohn, who sat in on rehearsals. Meanwhile, the head censor, a proper Southern gentleman called Bill Tankersley, was based in New York.

"Tank" was a decent guy. I always sided with the talent, but I knew from experience that the best course of action with Tank was to bring him in on a project as early as possible. That way he could track the progression of a scene or episode and he would have more of an understanding when it came time to make a decision. Tank tended to be more lenient that way, and he would sometimes come up with inventive workarounds that allowed borderline material to pass.

In this way, I had eased Tank through many a heated discussion with Herb Brodkin, such as how to show the birth of a baby on *The Nurses*, and I was sure I could do the same with the *Smothers Brothers*. But accommodation was not in the Smothers' vocabulary, particularly Tommy. The more the censors picked over their scripts the more the boys pushed back, especially from the second season onwards, when rival show *Laugh-In* appeared to be getting away with much more risqué and biting material on NBC.

But the friction had nothing to do with jealousy; it began long before *Laugh-In* appeared on the schedule. Indeed, just a couple of months after taking to the air, and while they were still in their tryout stage, the brothers submitted a sketch that lampooned the entire censorship process.

In a scene starring Tommy and the comedy writer Elaine May, two censors are depicted discussing changes they want to make to a film that includes the phrase "my heart beats wildly in my breast." The censors decide that the words "breast" and "heart" are both offensive and change the line to "my pulse beats wildly in my wrist, whenever I am near you." This proved a little too much for the censors, who banned the sketch outright.

Tommy was enraged. He took his fight to the press, allowing the script to be republished in The New York Times under the headline "The Sketch That Couldn't Be Done." From that moment on, any fight that he lost with the censors went straight into the next day's papers.

In one instance, Tommy revealed that the censors had deleted a sketch portraying President Johnson going crazy when he learns that the Soviet Union is 10 years ahead of the United States in the production of barbecue sauce. When Johnson's daughters, both fans of the show, read about this they implored their father to do something. The President called Paley, who in turn called me in the middle of the night and ordered me to make sure that the scene stayed in the show.

But the censors could not pick up on everything. The boys pushed some material through by force of will and some was cheekily ad-libbed. At other times references to drugs simply went over the censors' heads. Somehow Leigh French managed to maintain an ongoing sketch called "Share a Little Tea with Goldie," which was peppered with allusions to sex and mind-altering substances. The very term "Tea" referred to marijuana, and Goldie would always begin sketches with the catchphrase "Hi! And glad of it." I don't know how or why Tank never caught on, but he never said a word about it.

Although President Johnson may have stuck up for the boys in the barbecue sauce fiasco, it quickly became apparent that he was not a fan of the show. Joking about sex and drugs was one thing. But making fun of the Vietnam War was an entirely different matter. Frank Stanton was a very good friend of the President's and would often visit him at the White House. I am told that they sometimes watched the show together. Although Stanton never explicitly said that Johnson objected to the *Smothers Brothers*, I would often get a call after the show finished on a Sunday night asking who had vetted the scripts that week and questioning the decision to allow some of the more critical material. It was the only program that Stanton ever called me about.

"Listen, Mike," he would say. "Can't you do something about this show? Our boys are dying over there in Vietnam, and we should not be making light of it on a comedy-variety show on Sunday night."

My answer was always the same: "I will talk to the boys." But I never told them. Tommy knew the CBS hierarchy and the southern affiliates were going out of their minds. And he baited them. (It probably did not escape Tommy's attention that Lady Bird Johnson owned CBS's Austin affiliate, KTBC Television.) Meetings often devolved into shouting matches. No one could tell Tommy and Dicky what to do. And the more popular the show became, the more Tommy's ego grew. Listening to the advice being flung at Tommy and Dicky was like standing behind a Degas or a Matisse surrounded by kibitzers telling them not to draw such funny pictures.

It was Dicky and Tommy's misfortune to land at CBS during the network presidency of Tom Dawson, a former vice president in charge of sales who had taken over from John Reynolds in December 1966. As with Reynolds—and Schneider before him—Paley's idea was that Dawson should allow me to deal with programming while Dawson concentrated on broader issues.

But Dawson was not the sort to allow his executives to make decisions for themselves. Soon after the *Smothers Brothers* hit the schedule in early 1967, Dawson created a new position, "vice president in charge of administration," and appointed Bob Hoag to the post, stationing him on the West Coast. Hoag was to report directly to Dawson, and Perry and I saw him for exactly what he was, a Dawson plant to keep an eye on our programming decisions. Nice enough guy that Hoag was, Perry and I pulled all sorts of stunts to make life uncomfortable for him, including calling last-minute meetings to which he was not invited and Perry overruling and undermining him at every opportunity.

As the controversy around the *Smothers Brothers* gathered pace, Dawson decided that he could do what no man had so far accomplished. He would fly to the West Coast for a sit-down chat with the boys and set them straight. I called Tommy immediately.

"Tommy," I said. "Tom Dawson would like to come out and meet with you. He would like to have a personal conversation about the way the show's going. I think he's got some advice for you."

"I'd just love to see him," Tommy said. "Bring him over."

By now, Tommy and Dicky occupied the penthouse apartment at Television City that had once been used by Danny Kaye. When Dawson, Perry and I arrived, Tommy looked happy and relaxed. There was a delicious smell of baking in the air. And after Tommy had welcomed us in and offered us drinks, he emerged carrying a plate with a napkin over it.

Dawson walked over to Tommy and put his arm on his shoulder. "Tommy, I'd like to talk to you as a father…"

"Of course," Tommy said. "Would you like one of my brownies?"

Perry and I looked at each other. Dawson already had the brownie in his hand and was taking a bite. We both politely declined.

Now, Dawson may have had a bad plane ride or perhaps there was something in his food earlier that day. But within a short period of time he started to look a little nervous and bleary eyed, his speech became incoherent and we had to cut the meeting short. Tommy kept a straight face but there was definitely a twinkle in his eye.

Perry and I left with a very apologetic and red-faced president. Tommy never owned up to spiking the cookies, but whenever Perry and I called afterwards, we would always ask how his brownies were coming along, and he would reply, "Oh, my brownies are just wonderful. I love making brownies."

Tommy never had any trouble with Dawson again. But the show continued to attract unwanted attention. With the exception of my years under Jim Aubrey, I would say the *Smothers Brothers* posed the greatest pressure of my career. I was always worrying about what would be in the show, who would be on the show and what program practices would make of it. It was a constant battle and it never stopped.

In the fall of 1967, at the start of the second season, the boys invited the folk singer Pete Seeger to be a guest on their show. Seeger was a controversial personality. During the 1950s he had been accused of being a Communist sympathizer and had given evidence before the House Un-American Activities Committee. A decade later he was still blacklisted within the industry. When news broke that he was to appear on *The Smothers Brothers Comedy Hour*, I received 30,000 letters of protest. Nevertheless, the taping went ahead.

Meanwhile, the brothers put poor Perry Lafferty through hell. He could look and listen in on rehearsals via an intercom system in his office at Television City, and I understand he almost had a heart attack during the taping of the Seeger show when the singer finished off his act with a new song "Waist Deep in the Big Muddy." The song told the story of a platoon captain during World War II, who drowns after his commanding officer forces a group of men to ford a river that's too deep. There was no escaping the fact that the song was an assault on Johnson's handling of the Vietnam War and a direct attack on the President, especially the sixth verse, which broke away from the retelling of the story with the lines:

> *Well, I'm not going to point any moral;*
> *I'll leave that for yourself*
> *Maybe you're still walking, you're still talking*
> *You'd like to keep your health.*
> *But every time I read the papers*
> *That old feeling comes on;*
> *We're -- waist deep in the Big Muddy*
> *And the big fool says to push on.*

Perry tried to persuade Tommy and Seeger to perform something else or to cut the sixth verse but they refused. There were many anxious phone calls and Tank was brought in. The brothers left us with no choice but to cut the song entirely from the show. Naturally, Tommy and Seeger ran to the papers. The ensuing publicity and allegations of censorship caused quite a headache. And in the end we relented and allowed Seeger back on the show in February 1968, when he performed the song in full, to little outcry.

It may seem now that we were being overcautious. But these were the days when you could not say "hell" or "damn" on television, when you could only show a husband and a wife at nighttime in twin beds with a table and a lamp separating them. There was no precedent for glorifying sex and drugs on television, let alone insulting a sitting President. Sure, the movies and theaters were more lenient. But this was television, in those days possibly America's most conservative art form. And the country was in the grip of a political and a cultural revolution. At the start of 1968, the Vietcong launched the Tet Offensive, and the nightly news was saturated with images of dead and wounded on both sides. In April, Martin Luther King was assassinated. In June, Bobby Kennedy was killed.

Over the months I got letters from all sides, some saying keep the *Smothers Brothers* on the air and others demanding I take them off. I got letters from soldiers in the field who said they were thrilled with the show, and letters from soldiers accusing me of being un-American.

At the Democratic Convention in Chicago that summer, there was rioting on the streets and chaotic scenes within the convention hall itself. The *Smothers Brothers* made light of the chaos by overlaying television pictures of the violence with Harry Belafonte singing "Don't Stop the Carnival." The censors cut it.

But in the fall of 1968, the censors passed a sketch by the comedian David Steinberg in which he dressed up as a priest and delivered a mock sermon about God playing a prank on Moses. The network received thousands of complaints.

By now the pressure on the network was immense. Some of the affiliate stations were going crazy, and a dozen or more threatened not to carry the show. Stanton called me into his office and told me to pass on a message to the *Smothers Brothers*: From now on they were to send a tape of the show each week ahead of time so that it could be screened for the affiliates to decide whether or not to broadcast.

So began the weekly ritual of waiting for the tape of *The Smothers Brothers Comedy Hour* to be flown in from the West Coast. It was like something out of a James Bond movie. The tape would be stored in an attaché case and given to CBS employees who were making a trip that week. I was a bag of nerves, constantly awaiting both the tape's arrival and the affiliates' reaction.

As the pressure mounted, Tommy became ever more strident. The show took on an increasingly political tone and, to my mind, it lost some of its humor. The ratings began to slide, never something I wanted to see with any of my shows but particularly hurtful considering the brothers had been doing so well.

I had other problems too. Tom Dawson did not like me. Not only was I making all the programming decisions but I was also one of the most recognized names at the network. I had contacts at The New York Times, Variety,

TV Guide and The New York Post. And I was constantly upstaging him in the press, announcing deals and shows. In 1968, I heard rumors that he was looking to replace both me and Perry. One source was a projectionist who was in a room during a screening at which just Dawson and Paley were present. At the end of the screening, the projectionist told me, Dawson turned to Paley and said: "Mr. Paley, I've got to talk to you about Mike Dann. He's really not holding up. His name and picture are in the papers all the time. Everybody talks about him. I don't think he's very good for the CBS image."

To which Paley replied: "You know, Tom, you're absolutely right. He's got those problems. But how come we're always so successful in programming?"

And that was the end of discussion.

Luckily for me, Dawson's position was tenuous. In 1967, he had made the clumsy mistake of canceling one of Paley's favorite shows, *Gunsmoke*, *without telling the boss*. The program, then in its 12th season, was lagging in the ratings on a Saturday night, and Dawson probably made what he thought was a sound decision to cut it—but not without Paley's permission.

Perry had already informed the cast and crew that their contracts were up when Paley called from Lyford Cay and I gave him the news. His response was typical for its understatement: "I don't think that's such a good idea." A few days later he called again to *suggest* that *Gunsmoke* should return, but on a different evening. It ran on Mondays for another 10 years.

But I did not always have the golden touch either. In the winter of 1968, the 13th season since NBC had topped the ratings, the peacock network pulled ahead of us in the numbers. At one point it looked as though we were out of the race, and it took a good deal of midseason rejigging on my part—and a little bit of luck—when we came away with a slight advantage over our rivals.

With our dominance looking shaky at the beginning of 1969, anything could have happened. Fortunately, it was the departure of Dawson. In February 1969, just one month after Richard Nixon was sworn in, CBS found itself with a new president. Dawson was shunted sideways to become assistant to Jack Schneider, who was by now CBS Corporation's executive vice president, and Frank Stanton named Robert Wood the new president of the CBS network. Neither of these changes boded well for Dick and Tom Smothers.

The Nixon administration promised an even more conservative approach to the broadcasting industry, lambasting the loose morals and low standards that pervaded television. Meanwhile Bob Wood, the fourth network president I would report to in almost as many years, was determined to shake up CBS's programming strategy. Not that it stopped Tommy from yelling at Wood the first meeting they attended.

By March 1969, the atmosphere was unbearable. The censors were finding so many problems with the *Smothers Brothers* show that it was becoming increasingly difficult to get the tape to affiliates in time. At the beginning of the month we ran into our first major problem when the censors and Tommy had a fight over Joan Baez, who introduced a song on the show by dedicating it to her husband, David Harris, who was about to start a three-year jail term for refusing the draft.

"If you do that and you do it up front, over ground, then you are going to get busted," Baez said, rather innocently, I thought. But it was too much for the censors, who cut the entire introduction so that all the audience knew was that Baez's husband was going to prison, with no explanation given for the cause.

By the time Tommy agreed to the cuts, the censors had found more problems and, with time running out, we had to pull that week's show and substitute a two-month-old rerun. Naturally, the boys were livid. But they eventually calmed down and the Baez show ran at the end of the month—with the censors' cuts implemented.

Meanwhile, the brothers were fixated on their April 6 show, where they planned to bring back David Steinberg to perform another sermon, which was sure to be just as offensive as the first. I can still remember clearly—it was a Tuesday morning when I called Perry.

"When do I get the film?"

"I don't know. Tommy is looking for locations in San Francisco for another shoot. I know he's already finished the last episode. He has the film, but…"

"Just find Tommy. Try to locate him in San Francisco. Go to San Francisco yourself and find him if you have to, or send someone else. But find Tommy and find that film and get it to me as fast as possible."

Wednesday came and went with no sign of the show. On Thursday, Bob Wood called, saying he was holding an emergency meeting with CBS deputy general counsel John Appel at 3 o'clock that afternoon.

When I arrived in Wood's office, Appel was already there.

Bob turned to me and said, "Mike. Do you have the tape?"

"No," I replied.

Appel looked elated. "We got them!"

"What have you got?" I replied. But I already knew. CBS had been looking for an excuse to get rid of the brothers, and now it had one.

The tape arrived on Friday and, sure enough, Steinberg's sermon was deemed too offensive by the censors. The following Monday, Tommy arranged for a private screening for a group of a reporters at The Four Seasons in New York. Not only did the reporters find the episode inoffensive, they also declared it one of the brothers' best shows, making CBS look like a dictator for censoring the program as well as a putz for pulling it. To make matters worse, Tommy bad-mouthed CBS to the press. Although we had signed the brothers for a fourth season, it was obvious that the relationship was over. The show was canceled.

Though its numbers were occasionally poor—some weeks it fell out of the top 40—the cancellation of *The Smothers Brothers Comedy Hour* was a significant loss to the network. It highlighted the overzealousness of our censors, especially in comparison to NBC, which continued to let *Laugh-In* push the bounds of decency. And it cost CBS a fair amount of prestige—the year *The Smothers Brothers Comedy Hour* was canceled it won an Emmy for best comedy writing.

But Dick and Tom were not through with CBS. They took the network to court and sued for breach of contract. When the case finally came to trial, almost five years later and after I left CBS, I appeared as a witness for the brothers, providing evidence that CBS was indeed just looking for an excuse to get rid of the show. The network was ordered to pay $766,000.

In the meantime, I was stuck with the problem of filling prime time at such short notice. Thankfully, I already had a program up my sleeve, the rural variety show *Hee Haw*, which I slotted in for the summer.

With the *Smothers Brothers* gone I could go back to fighting the usual fires, angry producers, indignant writers and directors, slighted starlets, internal power struggles, and the demands of an indecisive boss. About the only relief was the occasional appearance of an extraordinary visitor, like Chagall, or the British television entrepreneur Lew Grade, who would visit to discuss exchanging programs and ideas.

Perhaps the strangest guest of all around this time was the head of the Greek Orthodox Church, who made an appointment to see me in the late 1960s to complain about the negative portrayal of Greek characters on television.

After Madeline let the patriarch in, I adjusted myself behind my desk and swiveled nervously in my chair while he sized me up.

"Mr. Dann," he said. "The Greek people are a good people. We are a religious people. Yet on television screens in this country we are portrayed as thieves and murderers and mobsters. We must not have any more of this. You must stop it."

"Your highness, your goodness, your Greekness," I said, unsure how to refer to a Greek Orthodox priest. "Your honor, I have never thought of it that way, but you couldn't be more right. And I will certainly call my producers and writers and directors and tell them that the intolerance towards any race, creed or color, particularly Greek, must and shall stop, and will not be tolerated on the CBS television network."

The patriarch smiled. "Mr. Dann, you are a good man," he said. "And I will respect what you said."

He was about to get up and leave, when I said, "Your holiness, I was just wondering, have you ever seen a picture called *Never on Sunday?*"

Now, *Never on Sunday* was a black-and-white film, directed by Jules Dassin, about a Greek prostitute and an American who became friends in Greece.

"Oh, it was a beautiful picture," the patriarch said. "The mountains and the waters and the music."

"But the lady"—I didn't want to use the word prostitute—"she was not the type of character your holiness would like to see on the screen as a Greek role model, now is she?"

"How right you are, Mr. Dann." The priest paused and thought for a while. "It would be much better if she was a shop girl or flower seller or something like that."

"Precisely," I said. "And that is just the kind of correction that Mr. Dassin would no doubt love to hear. In this one meeting, your holiness, you have solved two problems. You have improved an already wonderful picture and you have shown me what my responsibility is as head of programming for this network."

"Mr. Dann," the priest said as he offered his hand for me to kiss, "We have much in common." And he swept out of the room.

16.

100 Days That Shook TV's World

"Television has no subscribers, no income except from advertising. Advertisers put their money where the audience is and Mike Dann must deliver that audience. That's what television is all about today—delivering large audiences. Mike Dann does it better than anybody in the history of the business."
– Fred Friendly, New York magazine, September 1, 1969

The 1969 season began like any other, with angst-ridden days and sleepless nights as I fretted over the ratings. I was in my office every morning by 8 and usually home by 9, where I would end the day by putting in a call to Hollywood around 10 to find out what problems had transpired during the day's shooting. The new schedule looked solid enough despite losing *Gomer Pyle* after Jim Nabors decided he wanted to try his own variety show and dropping *Gentle Ben* (I got hundreds of letters for that decision—but the numbers proved he had lost his appeal). Other than that we had a number of decent pilots, including a strong new comedy *The Governor and JJ*, and some solid pre-existing programs that I had moved into alternative time slots in the hope of bumping up the figures even more.

The major scheduling problems of the season had been prime time Thursday, Friday and Sunday. NBC's *Daniel Boone* was strong on Thursdays, so I shifted two of our big guns, *Family Affair* and Jim Nabors' new variety show, into the slots opposite. To replace *The Smothers Brothers* on Sunday nights I signed a new variety show starring the African-American singer Leslie Uggams to go head-to-head with *Bonanza*. And on Fridays, opposite NBC's popular *The Name of the Game*, I stacked up an impressive line of comedies, *Get Smart*, *The Good Guys*, and *Hogan's Heroes*.

Signing *Get Smart* had been one of my toughest battles in the run-up to the new season. It had been a hit show on NBC for about four years until 1969, when its ratings dipped and the network decided to cast it, and its star Don Adams, aside. At the time, I desperately needed a comedy show for early Friday night, and when Ted Ashley told me that *Get Smart* was in play I jumped at the chance. At first Don Adams, who was a part owner in the show, was overjoyed to join CBS. But when NBC heard that he was going to switch channels they tried to tempt Adams back with an offer of six specials and a new variety show for the forthcoming season.

Ted called around 2 a.m. to tell me that Adams had decided to stick with NBC. So I ran downstairs in my pajamas and put a call into Adams in Hollywood.

"Don," I said. "You can't just drop a hit show like *Get Smart*." My voice was already starting to rise to a screech. "The American public won't stand for it."

I told Adams that the only star who ever quit a hit show and did not live to regret it was Jackie Gleason.

"I'm going to put you in unopposed on Friday at seven thirty," I said. "You'll be huge."

But Adams said he was not so sure. He said he wanted to have a think about it, that the variety show could be a good change for him and that he liked the idea of doing a half dozen specials. I would not give up.

"Look, Gleason quit three hit shows and survived. But look what happened to everyone else. Look what happened to Judy Garland. She was a star and she didn't last one season with her own variety show. *Get Smart* is not over. NBC made a mistake canceling the show and they are making a mistake with the variety idea. You're not ready for that yet. The American public isn't ready either. They want *Get Smart*."

I begged a second-rate comic to come work for me, not because I thought he was any good but because I needed a show at 7:30 on Friday, and *Get Smart* was better than any pilot I had. I don't remember at what price we started out, but I do remember that I finally hooked Adam for $3.5 million. He caved around 5 a.m, said he would talk to his people and get back to me with a firm commitment later that day. But I knew I could not allow him that much time to change his mind again, especially as NBC was sure to up its bid.

"Look, Don, I can't do that. Either you give me a firm commitment, a signature, first thing in the morning or our offer is off the table and we go with someone else."

There was a pause.

"Okay, I'll sign."

"That's wonderful, just wonderful."

It was already too late to go back to bed, so I had breakfast and went into work a little earlier than usual.

Around lunchtime I got a call from the West Coast confirming Adams had locked himself in. Never one for understatement, I immediately called The New York Post's entertainment columnist Leonard Lyons and told him that the

1969 season would undoubtedly be the most important yet—both for me and for the network—and that signing *Get Smart* could have been the biggest risk of my career. Then I dashed out of the office for a lunch appointment at La Caravelle with Sol Hurok.

At the start of that fall, CBS had won 14 seasons in a row, and each one of them had taken their toll on my health and on my personal life. By 1969, my marriage was all but over. It was one of the reasons why I left for work so early and came home so late. Weekends were often spent on the phone to Paley or arranging deals. I lived for my trips to Hollywood.

Among the inhabitants of the executive suites of the television industry, monogamy was the exception rather than the rule. Frank Stanton may have led an upstanding and somewhat dull life. But everyone else was dating: broads, actresses, secretaries, waitresses. I was no different. And neither was Paley, possibly the most notorious womanizer of them all.

Paley loved coming out to Hollywood to look at the pilots and the girls. His wife at the time was Babe Paley, one of the most beautiful women I have ever known. Babe was the youngest and prettiest of the "fabulous Cushing sisters," the daughters of the renowned neuroscientist Harvey Cushing. The girls had been raised to marry well, and Babe's current and former in-laws included an Astor and a Whitney. Meanwhile Babe herself was one of the most elegant, stylish and sophisticated, not to mention glamorous, women of her day. She and Paley had a strange relationship. I was never invited to their mansion at Kiluna Farm, but I often saw her at social functions where she would put her arm around me and, nodding towards her husband, say, "Mike, how do you stand him?"

When Babe Paley put her arm around you, it felt as though the whole room was looking at you. She was that perfect. I was used to gorgeous women draping themselves over me, but when Babe touched me I became so nervous. Not only was she one of the most attractive women I had ever known, but she was also the boss' wife.

Despite Babe's beauty, nothing could stop Paley from fooling around. Hollywood stars—famous women—would confide in me at dinner parties, giggling, "Oh, I love Bill. He's such a dear. He's such a fun guy to go out with." I remember once getting into an elevator at the Beverly Hills Hotel at about 2 in the morning with a girl I was seeing, only to be confronted by Paley standing there, stock still, with a lady friend of his own. We did not say a word to each other, not even to nod or say hello. I just pressed the button for my floor and stared at the back of the doors, wiggling my foot impatiently until the elevator journey ended and I got out on my floor, leaving Paley and his lady friend to continue on to his. It was never mentioned after that.

My private life was in turmoil. And so was my work life. As the 1969 season unfolded, it became increasingly apparent that my schedule was being rejected by the American public. Week by week, time slot by time slot, we were losing ground to NBC. *Leslie Uggams* failed to live up to expectations on Sundays, so I dropped her. I shifted the *Glen Campbell Goodtime Hour* from Wednesdays at 7:30 p.m. into the time slot opposite *Bonanza* and brought *Hee Haw* in to fill the empty Wednesday time slot. But it still was not enough.

My signing of *Get Smart*—and blabbing about it to The New York Post— also backfired. When the ratings came in the numbers were terrible. And my enemies at NBC could not contain their glee, particularly Paul Klein, NBC's vice president in charge of audience measurement. Klein and I had fought very public running battles in the past over scheduling and ratings. And when I arrived at the office one morning in the fall of 1969, I found a home-made funeral card, with a clipping of my Post article bragging about *Get Smart*, waiting on my desk.

Let Klein have his little joke, I thought. We were only weeks away from an episode in which Maxwell Smart was due to become a father. And as I knew well, babies were sure to boost the ratings. When the numbers came in, they did just that. But a few days later I received another note from Klein. This one read: "Pray for Mike Dann's babies."

I had enough to worry about with pressure from Paley and Wood about our poor numbers without becoming embroiled in a letter-writing contest with Klein. But I was not going to let him have the last word, so I just scrawled on the back of the note that Klein had no need to worry about my ability to feed my kids and told Madeline to see that it reached him.

A couple of days another note arrived from Klein. "I wasn't worried about you feeding them. I was worried about you eating them."

"Schmuck," I thought. "I don't have time for this."

Indeed, I did not. As if the ratings were not problem enough, after one year as president of the network Bob Wood decided it was now time to flex his muscles. No president since Aubrey had pushed through a schedule over my recommendations. And when Wood took over in early 1969, the 1969-70 schedule was all but set. But in late December, as we trailed NBC in the numbers and looked ahead to the 1970-71 season, Wood began to assert control. During January and February of the following year, just as I embarked on the battle of my career to salvage the ratings for the 15th year in a row, he launched a massive assault on my scheduling philosophy. At the programming meetings that February I conceded that a number of shows, including *Get Smart*, would have to be dropped. But I told Paley and the others that I was confident we had a good enough crop of pilots to fill the gaps and to win 1970-71.

For Bob Wood winning the numbers was no longer enough.

By the late 1960s demographics had become an obsession on Madison Avenue. The raw numbers were no longer as important as who was watching. When I took my programming ideas to our vice president for sales, Frank Smith, for one of my usual one-on-one chats ahead of the scheduling meetings, he told me that he could not support my proposals. Frank said his sales staff were struggling to sell some of our top shows, like Jackie Gleason and Red Skelton, whose audiences were skewing older with each passing year, and that he had told Wood as much. Entering the scheduling process for 1970-71 I broke one of my cardinal rules: I attended a meeting without first being sure of the outcome.

During that February I urged Paley to ignore demographics while the ratings were so tight. I told him we had a very good chance of winning the following year if we held onto our biggest shows and brought in a few pilots. But Wood would have none of it. Backed by Smith and Jack Schneider, he told Paley that our audience was simply too old and that we had to start appealing to younger viewers. Wood advised Paley that we had to sacrifice our hits, *The Red Skelton Hour*—a top-10 show—*The Jackie Gleason Show*, and *Petticoat Junction*. To my horror, he even suggested that we could afford to lose the ratings if we had to, because the gain in revenues on the back of a younger audience would offset the loss.

By now I was going crazy, though I tried my best not to show it. I told Paley that those shows formed the backbone of our prime-time schedule and that removing them put our ratings supremacy in extreme jeopardy. Even if they were not selling as well as we hoped, they maintained the network's aura of invincibility. And they drew vital eyeballs that stayed with the network for the rest of the evening, especially Skelton on Tuesday nights. If we cut these winning shows, I told Paley, the 1970-71 season could be lost before it had even begun.

In the past, Paley had sided with me against presidents Schneider, Reynolds and Dawson. But this time he overruled my protests and conceded that the three shows would have to go.

I should have read the warning signs. For the first time since the departure of Jim Aubrey, the balance of power at CBS was tilting back towards the network president.

But I was too focused on the immediate problems of the 1969-70 ratings disaster to pay attention. I was scared stiff that I was about to lose the current season. For as the scheduling arguments were taking place, NBC was pulling even further ahead in the ratings.

I always firmly believed that if you live by the sword, you die by the sword. Getting fired because of the numbers was probably the most honorable way to go. But the shame of being responsible for the end of CBS's dominance, after more than a decade at the top, spurred me to take the most drastic measures possible to salvage the season.

In January of 1970 my wife and I were barely speaking, and I had not slept properly for a couple of weeks. Although Dr. Fisher had increased my medication I was still nervous, jittery and prone to outbursts that were sometimes rude and uncalled for. Everything was on the line, my career and my reputation. That was why Operation 100 was so necessary.

Nothing like Operation 100 had been tried before in television and nothing quite like it has been tried since. On January 10, I stood in front of my team on the East Coast, including Fred Silverman and another close friend and colleague, Irwin Siegelstein, and I told them that we were going to rip up the schedule and start again from scratch.

"We've got one hundred days to catch NBC and we're not going to do it with this schedule," I said, my throat tightening as my voice rose. "So I want every idea you have, every day, from now until April, to make us win. I don't care who you have to call. I don't care what we have to pay—within reason. I've talked to Bob Wood and he is with us on this. Well, what are you waiting for?"

The 100 Days was a massive gamble. It was costly. It was conspicuous. And it risked the network's reputation as well as my own. While I was giving my speech on the East Coast, Perry was doing the same with his people on the West Coast. Our plan was to find out as much as possible about NBC's offerings from February through April, and to counter-program the hell out of them. NBC made our task a lot easier, because they were so certain that they had won the ratings that they made no changes to their midseason schedule at all.

Nevertheless, the project was enormous. Because of time and budget constraints, many of the shows we brought in last minute were far from guaranteed winners—old *Dinah Shore* and *Andy Griffith* specials, a movie version of *Peyton Place*, and documentaries like *The Trail of the Feathered Serpent* and *The*

Incredible Auto Race. Unspectacular as some of these shows were, anything was better than strugglers like *Get Smart* and *Tim Conway.* And sold right, I knew they might just be enough to turn the ratings around.

It was an exhausting period, physically, emotionally, mentally. I brought the team together every day to run through program ideas and to come up with ways of pushing them to viewers. Fred Silverman put in a heroic effort and at the beginning of February I promoted him to become my second in command. By mid-February everything was ready. All the 100 Days needed was a little bit of theater. So I called Les Brown.

"Les? It's Mike. Are you free on April 24? It's a Friday."

"Mike, that's two months away. Of course, I'm free."

"Good. Then we'll meet for lunch at Caravelle?"

"Can you tell me what this is about?"

"It's a story. You'll find out."

I hung up the phone and dictated a quick letter: "Dear Les, today I will tell you how it happened. Cordially, Mike," adding a little personal flourish in pen: "I hope you enjoy this lunch as much as I will." I was going to give the letter to Brown at our meeting, but I needed a way to prove that it had been written in February, so I put it in an envelope addressed to "Les Brown c/o Mike Dann," and called Madeline into my office.

"Madeline, please have this letter mailed to our office today. Oh, and call Les Brown and reconfirm our lunch appointment for Friday, April 24. It's very important."

It was not hard to work out which shows to replace over the 100 Days. Our numbers were dire. *Get Smart* was a loser—we pulled it seven times over the next few months—as were sitcoms *The Tim Conway Show* and *To Rome with Love,* and the western *Lancer.* But once we had found replacements, promoting them became an enormous task. I would sometimes pull shows at the last minute. And I often had only a matter of weeks, even days, to tell viewers about our new offerings. The editor of TV Guide, which closed weeks in advance, gave me hell for messing with his listings. But what did I care? I was too busy trying to work out how to sell the shows.

In one instance, simply renaming a program seemed to boost its ratings. One of my personal picks for the 100 Day lineup was a documentary made for the National Science Foundation about a tribe of Eskimos. It was a great film but, as was to be expected from a government agency, it had a very boring title. So I changed the name to *Eskimo: Fight For Life* and it was given a big push. We were rewarded with almost 30 million viewers, about 40 percent of the audience that evening.

Another strategy was turning ordinary movies into event television. CBS already had a regularly scheduled movie night on Thursday and Friday, so we decided to run longer films over two evenings to build excitement. One such movie was *Peyton Place*, which scored almost 40 percent of the audience on both nights it ran. Another movie that did exceptionally well over two nights was Howard Hawks' *Hatari*, starring John Wayne, which got an even bigger rating than when it had first run on ABC. Even *The African Queen*, which had been seen dozens of times on local stations, attracted 30 million viewers.

But no program epitomized our promotional success more than *Born Free*. It was Fred Silverman's idea to run *Born Free* on a Sunday evening because, he argued, it was a kid's show, and if we put it in the right time slot the whole family would want to watch. I scheduled it for 7 p.m. And in the four or five days leading up to the show we promoted *Born Free* in three separate trailers. During the commercial break in weekday soap operas we played clips of the movie's drama and heartbreak for the housewives, in the evening we played clips of the hunting scenes and the action for the fathers, and on the Saturday morning before the show we played clips of the cute lion cubs in between the kids' cartoon shows.

The morning after *Born Free* ran I called the office early for the overnight numbers. More than 40 million people had watched the show, the biggest rating of the year and one of the biggest TV movie ratings in history. I got straight on the phone to London and bought the rights to the sequel, *Lions Are Free*, a TV movie that had been made for NBC. Because no one yet knew what a success *Born Free* had been, I bought *Lions Are Free* at a discount, a few hundred thousand dollars. When it ran on a Tuesday evening a few weeks later, we scored a bigger rating than when it had premiered on NBC years earlier.

But for all our success, the odds of pulling off a last-minute victory were still stacked against us. In order to win the season, we had to beat NBC by 2.4 million viewers in every prime-time slot between February and April—a total 500 million viewers.

Bob Wood may have played along. But I am sure that everyone, from Paley all the way down to Fred Silverman and even the reliable Perry Lafferty, thought I was crazy. Even I thought I was crazy. But I had nothing to lose. I had had enough of the pressure and the stress, enough of taking pills to help me sleep at night, enough of the fights with my wife and spending days and weeks away from my family. This was going to be my final roar.

By the beginning of March, the numbers were starting to look promising. What had seemed like a quixotic mission suddenly started to look like a possibility. Our researcher Arnie Becker drew up charts which showed that if we continued at our current pace we might just beat NBC. Suddenly all of the fear that I had kept bottled up inside me came pouring out. I had to find someone to share this moment with. That was when I placed the call to Les Brown to ask him to meet me in my office. The place where this story began.

17.

By the Numbers

"I don't care what kind of person Mike is in business or what he means to other people. I don't care whether he brings good or bad shows to television—all I would say about him is that he is an exciting person, and he was very kind to me and fun to work for."
– Former secretary, quoted in "The Business Behind The Box," 1971.

Les Brown may have been incredulous when I showed him how I was going to win the season. But I did not care. The important thing was that I achieved my goal. Week after week, NBC's lead narrowed. And as we entered the final weeks of the season it looked like we might just pull it off. Arnie Becker assured me that we could do it. Our charts and projections showed that we could do it. We had NBC on the ropes. Then, at the beginning of April, Paul Klein pulled an audacious stunt. He went to the media and announced that NBC would end its season early. It was a blatant attempt to alter the rules of the game to ensure that NBC would win.

I was enraged. After all that I and my team had gone through, Klein was trying to rig the result. If anything, it showed just how worried NBC was that they might lose. Thankfully, the industry ignored NBC's announcement. The race went to the wire. CBS won with a 0.1 lead in the season ratings. I was overjoyed. My strategy of the 100 Days was vindicated. CBS's position as the number-one network was secure. I was still a winner. Paley, Stanton and Wood congratulated me.

In the run-up to the affiliates convention that May, I was full of optimism for the season ahead. Having won the ratings, we could continue to present ourselves as the leading network, and the sales team could continue to command top dollar. Our affiliates could be confident that CBS's schedule was solid. And as we prepared for the trip to L.A., I felt emboldened to push Wood to take a chance on a new comedy show brought to me by my friend, the agent Sam Cohn. The show, called *All In The Family*, was a U.S. version of a hit U.K. comedy called *Till Death Us Do Part*. ABC had screened it and balked at the controversial scripts about race and sexuality containing some pretty challenging language. I was certain it would be a strong show. But Wood said no.

The affiliates meeting was held in the Century City Hotel. And as usual, I was fully prepared for my performance as the entertainer. But when Bob Wood got up to speak, every ounce of energy drained from my body. Rather than celebrating our victory over NBC for the 15th year in a row, Wood tossed it out the window. He told the affiliates that CBS was no longer interested in just the bare numbers, that it was searching for programming that would bring in newer, younger viewers with fresher, more innovative forms of programming. It was a load of crap. And as far as I was concerned it was a public slap in the face after the exhausting and very public race I had just won for the network. When it was my turn to speak, I ran through the schedule as briefly as possible and then stepped from the podium. It was time to go.

The following month I quit the network. I took a $100,000 pay cut and went to work for Joan Ganz Cooney, the creator of Sesame Street, at the Children's Television Workshop. Cooney wanted to hire a number of producers to oversee different episodes of Sesame Street, and my first piece of advice was to find a single producer and stick with him to give the show some continuity. After that I earned my keep by selling the show around the world.

I was earning $25,000 a year, but for the first time in many months I was happy. Finally, I was free of the race for ratings supremacy. And I was working for a company, and a television show, which was doing good, teaching the basics of language and numeracy to children all over the globe. At CBS, meanwhile, Fred Silverman took over my job. Within a few years, CBS was no longer the number- one network in television. And it would never go on to repeat the success of the 1960s.

As well as working at the Children's Television Workshop, I was offered a position at Yale, where I taught a course about the "Wired Society." I warned my students that cable was just the tip of the iceberg. That one day the proliferation of delivery methods—what today we now know as the Internet and Blackberries and iPhones—would revolutionize the broadcasting industry. "The wired society is not like going from the propeller to the jet," I told them. "It is like going from the horse to the combustible engine. It is going to change society completely."

Despite those two jobs, I yearned to play an even bigger role in broadcasting. I set up a consultancy firm, and very soon I signed IBM as a client. Throughout the 1970s and 1980s, I worked with IBM's director of advertising, Charles Francis, to put on a series of big-budget spectaculars on commercial and public television: Rudolph Nureyev in *Sleeping Beauty, Baryshnikov on Broadway*— which won an Emmy—and George C. Scott in *A Christmas Carol*. The cost of these shows often ran into six figures and would be prohibitively expensive for one company to underwrite today. But IBM had the money then. And I was in heaven, truly free for the first time to make high-quality programming without the constraints of a network watching over me. My business expanded and I began consulting for a number of other companies. Steve Ross, of Warner Communications, hired me to help plan, launch and oversee early cable channels devoted to children's programming and music (called *Pinwheel* and *Sight on Sound*) that went on to become Nickelodeon and MTV. I helped Disney with its Epcot Center. And I advised the BBC as it expanded in the United States. I also traveled the world, dealing with Run Run Shaw in Hong Kong and Lord Lew Grade and Sir David Attenborough in the U.K. It was an exciting and highly fulfilling 30-year cap on an exhausting 22-year network career.

Today, looking back at that career, I have mixed feelings about what I achieved. I certainly was lucky to fall into an industry that I appear to have been made for. I doubt that I could have been more successful anywhere else. But my success as a scheduler came at a cost. There is no such thing as mass with class. And I won the ratings by serving the masses. That is what I am known for among many in the industry today.

But I did many great things, shows that I can be proud of—*The Defenders*; *East Side, West Side*; *Hogan's Heroes*; *Dick Van Dyke* and *Mary Tyler Moore*; even *All in the Family*, when it finally aired, was partially in response to my lobbying. The spectaculars too—*S. Hurok Presents, Death of a Salesman*, Hal Holbrook in *Mark Twain*, and Vladimir Horowitz. And later still, with IBM, some of the greatest public service specials of the 1970s and 1980s. Most of all, I can look back with pride that I was there at the very beginning, in 1948, when television really took off. I served in the trenches during television's most exciting decades. And I had the honor of learning from one of television's great masters, Pat Weaver, who taught me that culture and education in television are goals worth fighting for.

In my personal life too, I have much to be proud of. I have three wonderful, creative children—Jonathan, an award-winning documentary filmmaker, Patty, a successful author, and Priscilla, a clinical psychologist and freelance writer— and an equally talented generation of grandchildren who give me great joy. In 1973, I married for a second time, to Louise Dann, with whom I had 35 wonderful years, before she passed away in 2007. Today, at 87, I am married once more, to a loving and warm companion, Audrey Dann.

And I am still involved in the business too. Stirring up trouble at the networks and in cable. Advising, consulting—and, yes, still watching the numbers.

Acknowledgements

This book is the culmination of numerous interviews conducted over twelve months in New York City and Pound Ridge, NY. It has rewarded its authors with a lasting friendship and, we hope, resulted in a publication worthy of inclusion in the list of television histories. If it also helps people to relive, for just a moment, their favorite TV shows of the 1950s and 1960s, so much the better.

First and foremost, we would like to thank Peter Bernstein for introducing us and for sharing the knowledge and expertise that comes from a life spent at the top of the publishing industry. Without you, Peter, this book would never have been possible and we shall always be grateful.

We are also indebted to Jay and Beth Levine, who have done such a fine job of designing this book and bringing it to life in print.

Former friends and colleagues Fred Silverman, Jerry Leider, Charles Francis, Irwin Siegelstein, Dick Steenberg and Sal Ianucci, thank you for reminiscing about old times, and for reminding us of some of the anecdotes that have made this book richer.

Thank you also to those authors who have written with such passion and precision about the men and women who pioneered the early days of television. Harry Castleman and Walter J. Podrazik's encyclopedic Watching TV: Six Decades of American Television provided a much-needed jolt to the memory, and was an essential guide. Sally Bedell Smith's excellent portrait of William Paley In All His Glory brought back some wonderful—and painful—memories, as did Les Brown's detailed study of the 1969-70 season The Business Behind the Box. Pat Weaver's and Perry Lafferty's autobiographies were not only engrossing but invaluable.

On a more personal note, a great deal of this book was written during weekends in the country, where we were so well looked after by my housekeeper Erica and her husband Alex. Thank you for providing logs for the fire and delicious meals that helped us power through those long winter months.

Thank you lastly to our families, particularly our wives, who spurred us on when the task ahead seemed so great and who provided love, support, hope and encouragement throughout.

M.D. and P.B.
March 2009.

Printed in the United States
144575LV00001BC/1/P